Chocolate

How a New World Commodity
Conquered Spanish Literature

ERIN ALICE COWLING

HOW A NEW WORLD COMMODITY CONQUERED SPANISH LITERATURE

UNIVERSITY OF TORONTO PRESS
Toronto Buffalo London

© University of Toronto Press 2021
Toronto Buffalo London
utorontopress.com
Printed in the U.S.A.

ISBN 978-1-4875-0329-1 (cloth)   ISBN 978-1-4875-1765-6 (EPUB)
ISBN 978-1-4875-2720-4 (paper)   ISBN 978-1-4875-1764-9 (PDF)

Library and Archives Canada Cataloguing in Publication

Title: Chocolate : how a New World commodity conquered Spanish
 literature / Erin Alice Cowling.
Names: Cowling, Erin Alice, author.
Series: Toronto Iberic ; 63.
Description: Series statement: Toronto Iberic ; 63 | Includes
 bibliographical references and index.
Identifiers: Canadiana (print) 20210175141 | Canadiana (ebook)
 20210175745 | ISBN 9781487503291 (hardcover) |
 ISBN 9781487527204 (softcover) | ISBN 9781487517649 (PDF) |
 ISBN 9781487517656 (EPUB)
Subjects: LCSH: Chocolate – Spain – History – 17th century. | LCSH:
 Chocolate – Spain – History – 18th century. | LCSH: Chocolate – Social
 aspects – Spain – History – 17th century. | LCSH: Chocolate – Social
 aspects – Spain – History – 18th century. | LCSH: Food in literature. |
 LCSH: Spanish literature – Classical period, 1500–1700 – History
 and criticism. | LCSH: Spanish literature – 18th century – History and
 criticism. | LCSH: Spain – Intellectual life – 1516–1700. | LCSH:
 Spain – Intellectual life – 18th century.
Classification: LCC TX817.C4 C69 2021 | DDC 641.3/37409460903–dc23

University of Toronto Press acknowledges the financial assistance to its
publishing program of the Canada Council for the Arts and the Ontario
Arts Council, an agency of the Government of Ontario.

Canada Council   Conseil des Arts
for the Arts   du Canada

ONTARIO ARTS COUNCIL
CONSEIL DES ARTS DE L'ONTARIO
an Ontario government agency
un organisme du gouvernement de l'Ontario

Funded by the   Financé par le
Government   gouvernement
of Canada   du Canada

To Kyle, with love and chocolate.

Contents

Illustrations

Preface

Just before beginning my PhD, I was given the advice that most likely many a graduate student has heard: to pick a topic I loved for my dissertation, as no matter what it was I'd probably hate it by the end, so at least I'd love it for some of the time, rather than despise it all along. If I had to guess, I'd say the same goes for writing a book, and what's not to love about chocolate? I'm certainly not tired of eating it yet, anyway.

Chocolate is often depicted in modern popular culture as a food of love: romantic love, erotic love, even as a comfort for those who have lost love. Luckily, I have not lost any love while writing this book and am grateful for the love and support of my family and friends. Although I cannot name everyone without possibly missing someone inadvertently, there are three people who must be acknowledged for their love, support, and encouragement throughout the years. First, my husband, Kyle Davis, who is possibly sick of hearing about chocolate at this point, but who has graciously listened to me practise talks, discussed various ideas and theories as they occurred to me, and been unfailingly supportive of my career and all the interesting places it has taken us. Second, I must thank my parents, Patrick and Sarah Cowling, who have been my greatest supporters throughout my academic career, encouraging me to continue my studies, and modelling their zeal for travel, art, and literature – bugs I picked up from them at a young age and thankfully have not been able to shake.

In a way, this is a book I've been preparing to write since starting the master's program, even though I in no way mention chocolate in either my MA or PhD thesis. Much like my own studies, this book straddles historical research and literary analysis, with each chapter incorporating both, while also analysing the ways in which the political, medical, and religious debates of the day were represented in the literature. I am indebted to my MA supervisor, Dr Juan Luis Suárez, Western University, for encouraging me to combine my academic interests of history and literature, and for facilitating my first opportunity to spend time in the National Libraries and Archives of Spain. I'd also like to thank Dr Marjorie Ratcliffe, Western University, for her guidance (see the above advice, but also so much more) and as a truly remarkable example as a professor and mentor.

I am also grateful to Dr William Egginton, Johns Hopkins University, whose guidance as my PhD supervisor was fundamental in my development as a scholar. A small portion of this book, which now forms the basis for chapter 3, was first written as part of my thesis under Dr Egginton, and although it ultimately did not make the final cut of that project, the work I did at JHU under his direction remains a foundation for all that I do now.

As I move into the middle stages of my career – away from grad school and towards tenure – I have become more and more aware that the "Ivory Tower" should not be as lonely a place as it is often depicted. I have come to realize that collaboration and compassion are a necessary part of what makes academia work for me, and in that vein, I want to recognize four outstanding colleagues whom I am also privileged to call friends: Dr Glenda Nieto-Cuebas (Ohio Wesleyan), Dr Tania de Miguel Magro (West Virginia University), Dr Mina García (Elon University), and Dr Melissa Figueroa (Ohio University). Our research group, CIBRA (Collaboration Initiative by Baroque and Renaissance Academics), and frequent conversations, emails, texts, and collaboration over the years have helped shape me into the scholar I am today. Their advice, support, and friendship have been – and will continue to be – fundamental to my career and well-being. Each of them has read at least one of the chapters herein, and their feedback has been vital to the creation of the book you have in your hands now.

The research for this project has been supported by a number of institutions through both financial and other resources. I'd like to acknowledge the three institutions I've been fortunate enough to work at since finishing my PhD: Grinnell College in Iowa, Hampden-Sydney College in Virginia, and MacEwan University in Edmonton, Alberta. As a visiting professor at Grinnell College from 2013 to 2015, I had the opportunity to work with two students, Paige Erin Wheeler and Julia Marquéz-Uppman, on a mentored advanced project. As part of that project, they spent some time as my research assistants, finding articles and creating annotated bibliographies that helped me find a starting point for several projects, including this one. Hampden-Sydney College, where I was an assistant professor from 2015 to 2017, awarded me a Summer Research Fellowship that allowed me to take a trip to Spain in the summer of 2016 to gather many of the primary sources found herein. MacEwan University, my institutional affiliation as of 2017, also awarded me a Project Grant, which allowed for another research trip to Madrid to complete the work, as well as the support of an undergraduate RA, Ana Karen Rodas Garza, to work with me on some of the remaining translations in the spring of 2018. I am particularly proud to have had the opportunity to mentor these three talented undergraduate students as a part of this project, as they hone their research skills. The translations in this book by Rodas Garza will be noted as by RG, while those which we worked on jointly will be noted as by RG & EC. Any other translations without notation are my own.

Finally, I would like to acknowledge the many people who work at the Archivos Nacionales and Biblioteca Nacional de España, the editors and reviewers at the University of Toronto Press, especially Suzanne Rancourt, and the many people behind those people who may remain nameless and faceless to me but whose tireless efforts do not go unnoticed. Thank you for helping me find citations, double and triple checking my work, and all the other countless tasks without which my work would surely not be half as good as it is.

A note on source texts: while every effort has been made to uncover the numerous literary texts that mention chocolate, even in passing, it is always possible that some escaped my notice. They are abundant, as María Isabel Amado Doblas notes, given that the cacao bean and its related derivatives are the most cited products from the Americas during the period ("En el V centenario II" 358). There are also some whose reference to the drink is so brief and removed from the questions at hand that, in the end, it was not prudent to include them. That said, this study does its best to incorporate texts that pertain to the analytical categories laid out in the various chapters, and its author hopes that any oversight on her part will be taken up by future investigations. The language of source texts has been modernized to current Spanish spelling and punctuation, except in cases where it is necessary to conserve unusual spellings that contribute to the analysis of the text, or where the modernization would render the context moot.

Chocolate

Introduction

The Spanish conquest of the Americas was fraught with dissonance, at once repelling and attractive, similar yet different. It was this clash of cultures that birthed the Baroque, allowing for what is both different and same to coexist in a web of complexity, fraught with danger yet intriguing at the same time. In spite of overarching policies that would lead to the destruction of many Indigenous lives and customs, some cultural artefacts and practices survived the conquest and were, in some cases, even incorporated into the daily life of Spaniards and Spanish American Creoles.[1] Chocolate – as a drink – was one such product.

The year 1492 is well known around the world, and particularly in Spanish-speaking parts of it, for many reasons. For one, Antonio de Nebrija published the first book outlining the grammar of the Spanish language, dedicating it to Queen Isabel of Castile. He believed that she would need it, since "siempre la lengua fue compañera del imperio" ("language was always the companion of empire"; *Gramática*),[2] with empire being the cause that most would point to when asked the significance of 1492: the year Columbus sailed the ocean blue. What began as a somewhat misguided exploration for routes that could take him so far west that he would end up in the east was actually the start of the Spanish colonial era, in which the monarchs of Spain would hold so much territory that the sun would always shine somewhere within their grasp. It also introduced all kinds of new materials to the European consumer, from spices to precious metals and jewels, and, of course, the subject of this book, chocolate. It is hard now to imagine European countries without chocolate; Switzerland and Belgium are lauded for their decadent takes on the treat, and most visitors to Spain today would not leave without having *churros y chocolate* at least once.

It was not, however, love at first bite when the conquistadors tried chocolate in the New World. As the first and second chapters of this book will demonstrate, the preparation and serving of chocolate by the Indigenous peoples who introduced it to Spanish colonizers would be greatly altered in order for it be considered palatable by European standards, and it took more than a century after its introduction – two from the time of first encounter – for it to become widespread in Spain. This book proposes to look at the ways in which chocolate began to become construed in literature, and how the literary sources that encapsulate the incorporation of chocolate into Spanish society also reflected the anxieties of the governing bodies of the day.

It can be difficult to trace the exact trajectory of chocolate, given its ephemeral nature as a consumable product, but there are a variety of measures that can be used. For one, as new products were introduced into the European market, more and more secondary products became necessary, and the complexity of the global trading of goods increased. Nadia Fernández-de-Pinedo paints a picture of a highly globalized, commercialized, and interconnected world: "A noble could take a cup of coffee in a porcelain pot in Paris while a landowner in La Havana ate bread made from Castilian flour with cutlery from Sheffield and china from Mexico" (294). While this is an intriguing possibility, Fernández-de-Pinedo herself polemicizes the scene as set, since all kinds of factors – from wealth and social status to climate and religious beliefs – affected the adoption and maintenance of these newfound habits (294). The introduction of a new product such as chocolate – particularly at a time when it had to make a months-long, perilous journey to get to the new market – is often not an easy or smooth transition. It can take time and, as will be seen throughout this book, does not travel in a straight line. As Paula Findlen asserts:

> ... the global lives of things emerge within and at the interstices between local, regional, and long-distance trading networks. Much like the compass roses on a medieval portolan, networks only exist when a connection is made – no line touches another without a node that creates the point of contact which is also the moment of exchange. Each exchange becomes an opportunity to observe how things metamorphose from one society to another. The networks through which goods move are no more stable than the meaning of the things themselves. They can be redirected, extended, contracted, or even break down. They not only shape social relations and cultural preoccupations but tangibly transform the physical environment. (244)

For this reason, this book is interdisciplinary in nature, and it is necessary to include a wide variety of documents, from literary sources to historical papers. The study considers everything from poems to plays, medical and religious treatises to divorce cases, all of which weave together to demonstrate the slow, winding, but eventually steady movement of chocolate from New World to Old, and eventually from the homes of the nobility into the streets.

Chocolate was not the only new product vying for the hearts, minds, and stomachs of the citizens of the Spanish Empire. Coffee, tea, tobacco, and sugar all competed with cacao as the favoured import to show off one's social status.[3] Still, it took some time for these new trends to move from novelty to household good. Much like the volume *Global Goods and the Spanish Empire, 1492–1824: Circulation, Resistance and Diversity*, edited by Bethany Aram and Bartolomé Yun-Casalilla, this book does not limit itself to the traditional approach to the early modern period, which would normally consider the period from 1550 to 1700 as the delineating timeline. As Aram notes in the introduction to *Global Goods*:

> A sustained, explicit approach to the Spanish Empire and its sphere of influence, including collaborators as well as competitors, also enables researchers to chart very different responses to the same goods in distinct regions, at particular moments and among different social groups. This facilitates exploration of the prevalence and longevity of Old-World views, acknowledging the reluctant pact of adaptation to change among many Europeans and examining how different groups articulated and defined themselves by seeking and adapting or, on the contrary, resisting "American" products. (6)

This resistance, as will be discussed in chapters 4 and 5, can be traced to long-standing beliefs, religious and medical respectively, about the ways in which human bodies and souls function. Chapter 4, "Chocolate in the Church: Ecclesiastical Debates on Chocolate and Fasting," will discuss the ways in which the Catholic Church, and particularly the practice of fasting, influenced the popularity of chocolate. Chapter 5, "Chocolate: A Prescription for Health?" will look at medical theories of the time that held that foods, particularly those unfamiliar to a person, could have an effect on one's health and well-being, and colonial Spaniards went to great lengths to eat in ways that were familiar to them: "In the case of Spanish settlers, it was not simply that these foodstuffs helped maintain individual health. Such foods helped preserve their specifically *Spanish* complexion, despite their distance from the peninsula" (Earle, "Diet, Travel and Colonialism" 140, emphasis in the original).

As mentioned previously, the first two chapters will focus on the pre-Colombian history of chocolate and the introduction of chocolate to the early conquistadors, respectively. Chapter 3 will look at the economics of chocolate from its introduction to Spanish nobility up into the eighteenth century, to demonstrate the trajectory of chocolate from a specialized, exoticized product to everyday drink. Chapters 4 and 5, as mentioned above, will focus on religious and medical debates, and their appearance in the literature of chocolate. The last chapter will focus on the "darker side" of chocolate and the ways in which it was sexualized and demonized in historical and literary sources.

Finally, the epilogue will look at a modern source – the 2018 play *Mestiza* by Julieta Soria – that looks back at the colonial period through the eyes of one of the first children of the conquest, Francisca Pizarro Yupanqui, and which centres chocolate as an important part of the narrative. It might seem odd to include it in this book, which generally refrains from looking at sources produced beyond the mid-eighteenth century, but it is a good reminder that the Spanish conquest, and its effects on both sides of the Atlantic, are ever present.

CHAPTER 1

Pre-Columbian Conceptions of Chocolate

This book aims to discuss the relationship between chocolate and impe-rial Spanish society, through an interdisciplinary lens that incorporates both literary and historical documents written in the Spanish Empire from the time of conquest to the end of the eighteenth century. It might, then, seem strange to the reader that this first chapter will focus on conceptions of chocolate from prior to the Spanish-Indigenous encoun-ter. Yet it is in the pre-Columbian cultures that cacao was discovered and cultivated, and that chocolate as a drink was invented, and it is Amerindian societies that eventually introduced chocolate to the Span-ish conquistadors. Thus, we must analyse the cultural significance of chocolate to those peoples that originated it, to see how they transmit-ted their knowledge of chocolate to Europeans, with an eye towards the similarities – and differences – in their understandings and depictions of the beverage. Notably, all of the topics covered in the remaining chapters have clear antecedents in the pre-existing cultures of the "New World."

The early encounter between the European and Amerindian cultures was marked by misunderstanding. Beyond spoken language, there was a fundamental misinterpretation by the conquistadors that the peoples of what they called the "New World" were uncultured, lacking a writ-ten tradition that, to them, would indicate an educated, vibrant, and cultured civilization. It has long been maintained by prominent critics such as Walter Mignolo that the lack of books, as they were conceived of in Europe, created confusion among Spanish conquistadors, who did not understand non-alphabetic writings or the forms (non-book) used by Amerindians to transmit knowledge. This misunderstanding led to the loss of many pre-Columbian writings and oral traditions, leaving us with only those that were deemed worthy of preservation through transcription and translation, either by the conquistadors/missionaries from Spain or by elite members of Amerindian societies, educated, of course, by their colonizers. From those that remain, however, we are able to piece together some information regarding the culture and daily life of the various Indigenous groups from the pre-conquest period. In order to understand how the use and value of chocolate was communicated to the conquistadors and eventually translated into the social capital of Spain, this chapter will look at the preserved pre-Colombian sources and their interpretations by Spanish missionaries in the sixteenth century. Although there was some loss of sources, and literacies, because of the conquest, the Spanish invaders still had to incorporate linguistic and symbolic references in order to convert and conquer. Recent scholarship on pre-Columbian and colonial literacy has widened the definition of literacy to include a variety of sources and styles of communication.[1] This is important, as Kathryn Sampeck maintains, in order to open up "analytic space to those people at the margins of literacy, who did not read or write inscribed marks but who nonetheless made literacy part of their lives and in fact sustained practices that colonial officials worked hard to obliterate" ("Introduction" 410). Pre-colonial writing systems were also much more complex than they have been previously considered, with many recent critics including "graphical forms, postures and gestures, materials such as textiles, and crosses" as instruments of literacy (Sampeck, "Pipil Writing" 471). The material goods that can function within literacy are particularly of interest in the case of chocolate.

Although many written/graphic artefacts were destroyed, some material artefacts such as the ceramic vessels used in food preparation and consumption were preserved. At the Maya archaeological site at Colha in Northern Belize, researchers have found such vessels with dried, preserved cacao residue that dates back as far as 600 BC (Hurst et al. 289), demonstrating that chocolate was being produced and consumed for over two thousand years prior to contact with European cultures. Given the longevity of chocolate as a product, as well as the status of cacao in pre-Columbian cultures, one might reason that it would be a topic of interest in their literature. In spite of the tremendous loss of literary culture, we still have a few Maya sources that include references to cacao and chocolate, including the Dresden and Madrid Codices, the *Popol Vuh*, and the *Ritual of the Bacabs*.

Pre-Colombian codices are writings not written in an alphabetic language but instead in what the conquistadors conceived of as pictures or symbols. Since the Spaniards assumed them to be inferior because they could not read them, they relegated these pictographic inscriptions to the secondary tier of writing as outlined by Alejo Venegas:[2] if it is not of a book that helps humankind understand God, it must be influenced by demonic forces (Mignolo 70). Interestingly, as Timothy Knowlton points out, Maya communities adapted to alphabetic writings but still maintained their literary origins for some time, and are now considered to have been "characterized by 'script bilingualism' (Bricker 2000), or what Bender (2010) calls 'graphic pluralism': the coexistence of multiple systems of graphic representation," because they quickly adopted alphabetic writing but continued to refer back to previous graphic sources, and possibly even continued to produce new ones into the colonial period (583). Still, no more than four hieroglyphic Maya books are known to exist today, and none of those were produced post-conquest (Knowlton 583).

Dating from the thirteenth or fourteenth century, the oldest surviving Mayan text, known as the Dresden Codex, is divided into three parts, according to John E.S. Thompson: 260-day almanacs, 364-day counts for worship and divination, and astronomical and astrological materials used for divination (20). The first two parts make up the majority of the work and as such give us a look into the daily life of the Maya peoples. A search of the *Maya Codices Database* (Vail and Hernández) turns up twelve frames of the Dresden Codex in which cacao is thought to be represented. Of those, nine are interpreted as the cacao being used as an offering (see image 1.1), while the other

Figure 1.1 Dresden 10b, frame 2. Modified after William Gates, *The Dresden Maya Codex*. Publication 2. Maya Society, Baltimore, 1932. Courtesy of the Florida Institute for Hieroglyphic Research: Underworld god Kisin, holding what is thought to be a cacao plant (Vail and Hernández).

Figure 1.2 Madrid 52c. After Charles E. Brasseur de Bourbourg, *Manuscrit Troano: Etudes sur le système graphique et la langue des Mayas*. Imprimerie Impériale, Paris, 1869–70. Courtesy of the Florida Institute for Hieroglyphic Research: Deities at their wedding ceremony, offering each other honeycomb and cacao pods (Vail and Hernández).

three show it as sustenance for the gods. Both of these line up with what was observed by the first conquistadors who made contact with the Mexica and Maya peoples, and demonstrate that while cacao appeared frequently in daily life, its use was considered holy and special.

The Madrid Codex, another surviving Mayan text from approximately 1400, is also searchable in the *Maya Codices Database*, and contains six frames with references to cacao. The first of these, found in Almanac 52c, appears to depict a marriage scene between two deities, including offerings of honeycomb and cacao, an important part of pre-hispanic Mesoamerican wedding ceremonies (see image 1.2) (Vail and Hernández). Another depicts the Flower God (K'uh/Ahaw?

Nik) surrounded by cacao plants, possibly depicting a time of plentiful harvest. The last four, all found in Almanac 95a, depict deities in the act of bloodletting (via the earlobe), accompanied by other material objects that could be interpreted as offerings, such as cacao and incense. These four frames connect chocolate as an offering within sacrificial, religious ceremonies.

The codices are still very much a subject of interpretation and translation, as they were not written into an alphabetic language by either Amerindians or Spanish interpreters at the time of conquest. However, there were other books that for one reason or another were deemed "worthy" of being translated into a writing style and language more familiar to the conquistadors. One such book is the *Popol Vuh*, a text which transcribes the mythological and historical origins of the K'iche' people. It was written down in K'iche' using the Latin alphabet, which was then translated into Spanish some two hundred years after the first encounter between Amerindians and Spaniards as *Historias del origen de los Indios de esta Provincia de Guatemala* by a priest in the Santo Tomás Chichicastenango parish, Francisco Ximénez. We do not know the original author of the K'iche' version of the *Popol Vuh*; however, we do know that it was written down sometime after 1550, as that is the last date given in the chronological listing of their leaders. Nonetheless, many of the narrative episodes can be traced back to long before the arrival of the Spanish explorers, perhaps as far back as 400 BC (Coe and Coe 40). Although the translators of the English version preface their translation – originally printed in 1954 – with the assertion that the alphabetic K'iche' version had been lost, positing that Ximénez, upon copying and translating it, returned the book to its Indigenous owners and thus back to obscurity (Goetz and Morley xi), there is in fact a surviving version of the K'iche' text, alongside a Spanish translation by Ximénez dated between 1700 and 1703, housed in the Newberry Library, Chicago.

Unlike its codex counterparts, the depiction of cacao in the *Popol Vuh* is relatively benign. Rather than offering or sustenance for the gods, here it is one of the materials required to form and maintain human beings:

> Así, pues, encontraron la comida
> así, pues, entró en la carne del hombre creado
> > del hombre formado.
> El agua, pues, se hizo sangre
> > la sangre del hombre.
> Así entró por medio de Alom
> > K'ajolom, el elote.
> Así, pues, se alegraron, pues por el descubrimiento de la hermosa montaña, llena de dulzuras
> tupida de elotes amarillos
> > de elotes blancos
> > tupida también de pataxte[3]
> > de cacao
> > incontables zapotes
> > anonas
> > jocotes
> > nances
> > matasanos
> > miel. (Craveri 133)

And this was when they found the staple foods.

And these were the ingredients for the flesh of the human work, the human design, and the water was for the blood. It became human blood, and corn was also used by the Bearer, Begetter.

And so they were happy over the provisions of the good mountain, filled with sweet things, thick with yellow corn, white corn, and thick with pataxte and cacao, countless zapotes, anonas, jocotes, nances, matasanos, sweets ... (Tedlock 146)

Although many interpretations of this passage view it as a more commonplace rendering of cacao within the Maya literature, particularly in comparison with the Dresden and Madrid codices, I would argue that the joy with which the gods celebrated this discovery, one that allowed them to create human beings after their failed earlier attempts, demonstrates that, although allowable for human consumption, there is something special about this place and these goods that create and sustain life. Previous incarnations of human beings had failed, but the discovery of these other materials, the two cacaos, honey, and other local plants, allows humans to thrive. As David Freidel, Linda Schele, and Joy Parker note, the foods listed in the above passage are ones that are still staples of the region today (111). Although corn is the main ingredient necessary for human life in the Maya creation story, these other fruits hold importance for their proximity to the creation of the first four humans, and as continuing sustenance. Interestingly, it also places *pataxte* – a relative of the cacao tree that is often treated as indistinguishable from it – in the first position of the list of trees the humans found. Although *pataxte* has been ignored in favour of cacao, Johanna Kufer and Cameron L. McNeil argue that it was far more important than previously recognized in pre-Columbian Maya communities (104), and its specific inclusion here as a separate food that could sustain life demonstrates that importance.

The *Ritual of the Bacabs* comes to us from an eighteenth-century manuscript written in the Yucatec language, using the Latin alphabet. Although the manuscript itself is dated some 250 years after first contact with Europeans, its first English translator, Ralph L. Roys, posits that the material is most likely copied from "a much older manuscript, which might have been written during the first part of the seventeenth century, or possibly even earlier" (vii). Knowlton notes that the tropes found in the manuscript are most similar to those found in the Classical period (ca. AD 250–909), and posits that this "suggest[s] a continuity in Maya poetics enduring over a millennium"; however, given that there is no reference to the materials in any of the existing pre-Columbian texts, it is difficult to give a taxonomy of their origins (575–6).

The *Ritual of the Bacabs* is primarily a book of medical incantations, which makes use of the plants available in the Yucatan peninsula to aid the conjuror's request of the gods.[4] Roys assures us that medicine and benevolent magic were closely related in pre-Colombian cultures (ix). Although Roys's translation is a valuable source, I will hereafter cite David Bolles's 2003 edition, which uses both the Roys English translation and Ramón Arzápalo Marín's translation into Spanish as references, and includes copious notes on word choice and contextual information that helps interpret the incantations and their uses. For example, cacao and/or chocolate are mentioned four times in the Roys translation; Bolles, however, has six notes on chocolate that either add new possibilities of interpretation and/or complicate Roys's translation. According to Bolles, at least three of the incantations that include cacao or chocolate are for curing what he translates as seizures.[5] Other mentions of chocolate are within incantations against "snakes in the stomach," which seems to mean any kind of affliction thought to have been brought on by a curse made by an "h-menoob" or shaman using a rattlesnake as a familiar or medium (83n). Although the majority of the incantations in the *Ritual of the Bacabs* are meant to heal and not harm, the connection between chocolate, medicine, and magic is one that will carry over to Spanish cultural understandings of chocolate.[6] The inclination in Spanish society, however, is to consider any kind of magic or sorcery as potentially dangerous, and thus the associations with Indigenous magic do have some negative connotations, as will be seen in chapter 5.

Sophie and Michael Coe, in their extensively researched *The True History of Chocolate*, assert that chocolate was actually far less integral to Aztec society than has long been assumed:

There is a curious ambivalence in Aztec thought and culture regarding their two most important drinks, *octli* (the native "wine") and chocolate. This stems from an ambivalence in their society as a whole ... by the close of the 15th century Tenochtitlan and the other cities of the

Valley were rolling in luxury goods, and the elite class along with the warriors and merchants enjoyed a way of life that was unmatched in Mesoamerica. But there were heavy restrictions on the use and consumption of these luxuries, such as the rigid sumptuary laws about dress and ornament. There was, in fact, a strongly puritanical streak in Aztec life. (77)

Still, that does not exempt chocolate from appearing in the source texts. The Codex Barberini (or Badianus Manuscript), written down as we now know it in 1552, is an illustrated text that explains the proper uses of a variety of herbs and plants available to the pre-conquest Aztec people. Of the 118 plates, there are three illustrations of different parts of the cacao plant. Although, as will be seen in chapter 5, there were a variety of interpretations by Spanish physicians as to the medicinal effects of chocolate, the Aztec interpretation of the plant is fairly benign. In one case, the *cacauaxochitl* flower is mixed with other flowers and herbs to make a topical lotion which would cure injuries of the feet (plate 75, p. 270); the flower can also be crushed up with other herbs and flowers into a drink to treat fear and combat "mental stupor" (plate 98, p. 311n),[7] while *Tlapalcacauatl* or coloured cacao is mentioned in a list of "trees and flowers [used] for the fatigue of those administering the government and holding public office" (plates 70–1, p. 276). This use of the cacao tree intersects with the religious debate held in Spain, as outlined in chapter 4 which was mainly concerned with chocolate as an energy provider. Finally, one plate (plate 98) illustrates the use of the root to create a juice that cures mental stupors. None of the medicinal descriptions of the plant found in the Badianus Manuscript, however, make use of the bean as an edible substance, even though that is the part of the plant most used for making chocolate as it was introduced to sixteenth-century Spanish society. Still, as Emily Walcott Emmart points out in her English translation of the manuscript, the use of plants for medicinal purposes such as the treatment of fatigue shows the advanced nature of Aztec society:

> The recognition of fatigue as a disease by the Aztec native doctors is an indication of the degree of advancement of medicine in Mexico. The particular emphasis on fatigue "of those administering the government and holding public office" sheds light both on the attitude of mind toward fatigue and lack of vigor as well as the role of the public official of the Aztec empire before the Conquest. Nor was this ailment treated lightly. If one could judge from the length and the number of substances used, it was considered of greater importance than any other treatment in the text. (277–8)

Although the religious debates of Spain were concerned about the amount of energy one might receive from imbibing chocolate, as it would potentially break the fast, it is interesting to note that the Aztecs had also recognized this property of the plant but were in fact harnessing its power in a positive way, to cure fatigue. It is interesting to juxtapose the concerns of the two cultures. Where in Spain the religious leadership was concerned with those who would do too much on days of fast, in the Aztec empire chocolate was seen as a medicinal supplement to help government workers do more.

In spite of the acceptance of the drink as medicinal, it was still not considered suitable for daily, unbridled use, as Coe and Coe note, which may be attributed to the Aztec origin stories, as retold by Diego Durán, a Dominican friar who wrote the *Historia de Las Indias de Nueva-España y Islas de Tierra Firme* (1581), also known as the Durán Codex, which included Indigenous sources. He recounts the story of a mission undertaken by Montezuma I in search of Aztec origins. When they reach a mountain that they must climb in order to learn the truth of their ancestors, they meet an old man who will serve as their guide. With every step they take, they become more exhausted, while the old man seems to be able to practically fly. When he asks what they consume that makes them so heavy and tired, they respond that they drink chocolate:

> El Viejo les respondió: esas comidas y bebidas os tienen, hijos, graves y pesados y no os dejan llegar a ver el lugar donde estuvieron vuestros padres y eso os ha acarreado la muerte; y esas riquezas que traéis no usamos acá dellas, sino de pobreza y llaneza, y así dadlo acá y estaos allí, que yo llamaré a la señora destas moradas, madre de Vitzilopchtli, para que la veáis ... (*Historia* 1:223)

> The elder responded, "Such food and drink, my children, have made you heavy and they make it difficult for you to reach the place of your ancestors. Those foods will bring death. The wealth you have we know nothing about; we live poorly and simply. Give me your loads and wait here. I will go call the mistress of this land so that you may see her."
> (Heyden and Horcasitas 136)

Their offering to the wise woman of food and chocolate is met with similar disdain, and she warns them as they leave that they will never understand their ancestors or the magical place where they live so long as they burden themselves with foods that can damage them: "Mirad: todo ese daño os ha venido y se os ha causado dese cacao que bebéis y desas comidas que coméis; esas os han estragado y corrompido y vuelto en otra naturaleza; y esas mantas y plumas y riquezas que trujistes y de que usáis, eso os ha echado a perder" ("You have become old, you have become tired because of the chocolate that you drink and the foods that you eat. They have harmed and weaken you. You have been spoiled by those mantles, feathers and riches that you wear and that you have brought here. All of that has ruined you"; 226; Heyden and Horcasitas 138). In spite of such warnings, neither the Aztec peoples nor the Spaniards who first encounter chocolate seem to be able to resist it, even if the Aztecs themselves only imbibed on special occasions.

Although little pre-Columbian literature remains, the *Códices Matritenses*, compiled by Bernadino de Sahagún during his mission work in New Spain in the second half of the sixteenth century, do conserve a poem in Nahuatl, which Jacqueline de Durand-Forest includes in both the Latinized Nahuatl and a Spanish translation in her 1967 article "El cacao entre los aztecas." Originally titled "In cacayanamac" and translated as "El vendedor de cacao," the poem relates how different cacao sellers are either "good" or "bad" based on the form of chocolate they sell:

El buen comerciante de cacao
vende
(granos de cacao) gruesos
macizos
redondos
bien redondos
duros
seleccionados
escogidos.
…
El mal comerciante en cacao
(es) un engañador
él arregla el cacao
vende
cacao
verde ceniciento
cacao (asado) tostado
hinchado en el fuego
inflado en el agua
maduro (160–1)

The good trader of cacao sells (cacao beans) thick, solid, round, very round, hard, and hand-picked … The bad trader in cacao (is) a deceiver, he sorts out the cacao, sells cacao, ash-grey green cacao, (roasted) toasted, bloated in fire, inflated in water, ripe. (Trans. RG)

Thus, good sellers sell whole beans to show the buyer the quality of their goods, while bad sellers tend to trade in cacao that is already roasted and pulverized, so that the customer cannot inspect the quality in the same way. While the Spanish documents do not necessarily refer to the level of processing – since the chocolate must be processed and preserved to make the transatlantic journey – there were definitely different sources and qualities of chocolate that would fetch better prices, as well as merchants who attempted to defraud their clients, as will be discussed in chapter 3. Thus, the anxieties surrounding the quality and origin of chocolate are transferred across the Atlantic along with the product.

There are other sources from the early conquest period that could be discussed here, but I have decided to hold them for the next chapter. These include a variety of the conquest chronicles from the early conquistadors, including Hernán Cortés and Diego de Landa, as well as the official chroniclers of the crown such as Gonzalo Fernández de Oviedo, and missionaries such as Bernardino de Sahagún, who preserved and commented on Amerindian codices. I have chosen to leave these for a separate chapter because, although they are often based on Indigenous sources – particularly in the case of Sahagún – they are written through a very specific, colonizing lens that must be taken into consideration when using them as source texts. As can be seen, however, even in the fragmented documentation that we still have from the pre-Columbian period, there are connections that can be made to the religious, medicinal, and even commercial properties of chocolate as they were understood on both sides of the Atlantic.

CHAPTER 2

Encountering Chocolate: What Is It Good For?

The first Spaniards to encounter chocolate were also among the first to enter the New World. As such, they were soldiers, conquistadors, and missionaries, and their writings reflected their station and preoccupation. Rather than creating fictional accounts,[1] their aim was to report their findings back to the Old World, while also subduing and converting the Indigenous peoples and cultures with which they came into contact. Thus, the writings coming out of the colonial voices of the New World that include references to cacao and chocolate in the first fifty to one hundred years post-encounter tend towards the informative, repeating the information given to them by Indigenous peoples, describing the drink and plant in ways that might be relevant to their European audience, and detailing its daily and ritual uses. This chapter will look at the ways in which the historical documents – letters, chronicles, etc. – written for the purpose of informing the Spanish crown of the deeds and findings of the conquistadors and religious leaders in the New World comment on this new-to-them plant that would go on to become a very popular drink in Spanish society. These documents are, in some ways, a hybrid creation of the society for which the writers were recounting their findings and the culture about which they were writing. As such, there is an interesting cross-pollination between the cultural understanding of cacao from the perspective of the Indigenous peoples and its potential as an export from the newly formed colonies. Many of the writings of this period can be divided into four categories: cacao bean as currency; the use of the drink in ceremonies and as a gift; the cultivation of cacao trees and processes of creating the drink; and its use as a health supplement by the Indigenous peoples and consequent implications for the health of Spanish citizens.

The concept of beans as currency, or, at the very least, a valuable commodity, is known from the very earliest times of the conquest. Perhaps unsurprisingly, Christopher Columbus is considered the first outsider to come into contact with cacao beans, although it is less certain that he recognized them for what they were. According to Consuelo Varela Bueno and Manuel Alvar, Columbus himself mentions the drink unwittingly in the diary of his first voyage: "Echaban un grano en una escudilla de agua y bebénla, y decían los indios que consigo traía el Almirante que era cosa sanísima" ("They put a bean in a bowl of water and they drank it, and the Indians whom the admiral brought said it was very healthy"; Colón, *Textos y documentos* 94; Pérez Samper 25).[2] Fernando Colón's account of his father's life recreates a better-known encounter thus: "y muchas almendras que usan por moneda en la Nueva España, las que pareció que estimaban mucho, porque cuando fueron puestas en la nave las cosas que traían, noté que, cayéndose algunas de estas almendras, procuraban todos cogerlas como si se les hubiera caído un ojo" ("and they use many almonds as currency in New Spain, and they seem to think very highly of them, because when they loaded their things on the ship, I noticed that, as some of these almonds fell, they procured to pick them all up, as if one of their eyes had fallen out"; 275; trans. RG).[3] Although neither father nor son is known to have ever tasted the end product, the younger Columbus observes the potential value of the bean to the Indigenous community and recognizes its use as a currency, at the very least.

The understanding of the monetary nature of the cacao bean is also echoed by one of the Spanish soldiers supposedly accompanying

Hernán Cortés, known only as the "Anonymous Conqueror," as well by as the official chronicler, Gonzalo Fernández de Oviedo, and by several missionaries, including José de Acosta and Juan de Torquemada, both considered important chroniclers of their experiences as religious men in the New World. Both the "Anonymous Conqueror" and Acosta make note of the value of the bean in comparison with goods that are more understandably valuable to their European reader: "Estos árboles son muy apreciados, porque sus semillas son tenidas como la principal moneda que corre en aquel país, y vale cada una como medio *marchetto* entre nosotros, y es la moneda más común, aunque muy incómoda, después del oro y la plata, y la que más se usa de cuantas hay en aquel país" ("These trees are held in great esteem because the said grains are the principal money that passes in the land and each one is of the value of half a marchetto of our money. Inconvenient as this money must be, it comes after gold and silver and is the one most used by everyone in this land"; Conquistador anónimo 113; Saville 39–40). Acosta, writing some fifty years later, notes that while precious metals are used as ornament, they are never used as a monetary instrument; instead, trade is done through the exchange of goods or, in the case of Mexico, through the use of cacao beans as currency (144). How much cacao beans were worth, exactly, is difficult to determine, as the market fluctuated based on the year's harvest and on where it was cultivated and where it was being sold. The "half a marchetto," above, has since been valued at the equivalent of one Mexican cent per bean or approximately 535 beans per peso in 1875 by Joaquín García Icazbalceta (245n). Toribio de Benavente Motolinia, one of the first Franciscan missionaries sent to New Spain at the behest of Cortés, accounts for the value and counting system of cacao beans:[4]

Una carga tiene tres números, que los indios llama *xiquipilli*: vale e suma este número ocho mil, y una carga son veinte y cuatro mil almendras cacaos. A do se coge vale la carga cuatro o cinco pesos: llevándolo

la tierra adentro va creciendo el precio, y también sube y abaja según el
año: ca en buen año multiplica mucho, y con grandes fríos es causa de
haber poco, que es muy delicado. (85)

A load has three numbers, which the Indians call *xiquipilli*: this number
is worth and adds up to eight thousand, and a load is twenty-four thousand cacao beans. Where it is collected it is valued at four or five pesos:
moving inland increases the price, and it also increases or decreases,
depending on the year. In a good year, it multiplies a lot, and great cold
causes there to be little of it, because it is very delicate. (Trans. RG & EC)

Icazbalceta affirms that the "pesos" referred to by Motolinia are
"pesos de oro." Another source cites the price of a *carga de cacao* at
two hundred *reales*, but given that the letter is undated, it is difficult
to make comparisons (Acuña 269). Still, the value of chocolate – at
least, once the Spaniards arrived – can be inferred by the comparisons
made in the sources themselves, although we should note that the
sources that give these valuations are primarily from the European
perspective, as opposed to that of the Indigenous groups. The same
undated/unsigned letter notes that "una botija de vino vale una carga
de cacao" ("a cask of wine is worth a load of cacao"; 269) and that
wine was highly sought after by the Indigenous peoples, but that they
could not be trusted not to make a drunken spectacle of themselves,
in spite of Motolinia's assertion that wine – and particularly the state
of intoxication that it could create – was considered dangerous, and
overindulging dishonourable (550).

Of the conquistadors, Hernán Cortés is the most likely the first
to actually try the drink, along with several of his companions,
who also wrote their own accounts of the rituals they witnessed.
Cortés, in the second of his *Cartas de relación*, dated 30 October 1520, writes that cacao is among the provisions sent to him
by Montezuma: "y trajéronme diez platos de oro, mil quinientas
piezas de ropa, mucha provisión de gallinas, pan y cacao, que es

cierto brebaje que ellos beben" ("and they brought me ten plates of gold, one thousand five hundred pieces of clothing, many chickens, bread, and cacao, which is a particular concoction they drink"; 106; trans. RG), thus linking cacao to other esteemed gifts. This attempt to pacify Cortés strikes a balance between what the Spaniards were thought to desire – gold – and what was valued by the Indigenous people, as he later notes when discussing the planting and harvesting potential of the area: "estaban sembradas sesenta hanegas de maíz, diez de fríjoles y dos mil de cacao, que es una fruta como almendras, que ellos venden molida y la tienen en tanto, que se trata por moneda en toda la tierra y con ella se compran todas las cosas necesarias en los mercados y otras partes" ("there were planted seventy bushels of maize, ten of beans, and two thousand of cacao, which is a fruit like almonds, that they grind and sell and have so much of that it is treated as currency across the whole land, and with it they buy all things necessary in markets and other places"; 123–4; trans. RG). The Spanish government would have been aware by that point of the value and necessity of maize and beans both for the Indigenous populations and their own, but Cortés feels that cacao is both important and novel enough to merit an explanation beyond his previous mention of the drink.

Durán's account of the Spaniards' first introduction to chocolate is one that perfectly embodies the mixture of familiarity and Otherness that shapes the conquistador's understanding of the New World and its peoples:

Los indios las empezaron a probar y a comer de todo y como iban probando los españoles iban tomando de aquellas gallinas asadas y de aquellos guisados y de aquel pan y a comer con mucho regocijo y contento y con muchas risadas y pasatiempo; y venidos a querer beber del cacao que les habían traído, que es el brebaje preciado que estos indios beben, temieron, y viendo los indios que no lo osaban beber empezaron ellos a hacer la salva de todas las jícaras y tomándolas los españoles

bebieron el cacao, refrescándose con aquello, porque en realidad de verdad es bebida fresa. (*Historia* 2:7)

The two Aztecs tasted the different foods and when the Spaniards saw
them eating they too began to eat turkey, stew, and maize cakes and
enjoy the food, with much laughing and sporting. But when the time
came to drink the chocolate that had been brought to them, that most
highly prized drink of the Indian, they were filled with fear. When the
Indians saw that they dared not drink they tasted from all the gourds
and the Spaniards then quenched their thirst with chocolate and realized
what a refreshing drink it was. (Heyden and Horcasitas 266)

In the original, Durán seems to pass judgment as if he himself had
experienced the refreshing quality of the drink ("porque en realidad
de verdad es bebida fresca," which I would translate as "because in
truth it is a refreshing drink"), while the Heyden and Horcasitas translation ("realized what a refreshing drink it was") allows the unnamed
Spaniards to come to that conclusion. Although Durán does not detail
why the drink was held in such high esteem, he later mentions its use
in rituals, as a gift of welcome to important guests, and in funeral
rites, both to serve the guests and as an offering to the deceased.[5]

Cortés's companions also found cacao interesting enough to mention in their own accounts. Bernal Díaz del Castillo, for example,
mentions that Cortés is brought chocolate as a gift of reception (*Historia* 167), and makes the first reference to the purported aphrodisiacal effects of the drink – a perception that will be repeated in the
literature of Spain, as will be discussed in chapter 6, and persist long
after the Spanish Empire falls:

Mientras que comía, ni por pensamiento habían de hacer alboroto ni
hablar alto los de su guarda, que estaban en sus salas, cerca de la de
Moctezuma. Traíanle fruta de todas cuantas había en la tierra, mas no
comía sino muy poca de cuando en cuando. Traían en unas como a

manera de copas de oro fino con cierta bebida hecha del mismo cacao; decían que era para tener acceso con mujeres, y entonces no mirábamos en ello;[6] mas lo que yo vi que traían sobre cincuenta jarros grandes, hechos de buen cacao, con su espuma, y de aquello bebía, y las mujeres le servían con gran acato. Y algunas veces al tiempo de comer estaban unos indios corcovados, muy feos, porque eran chicos de cuerpo y quebrados por medio los cuerpos, que entre ellos eran chocarreros, y otros indios que debieran ser truhanes, que le decían gracias y otros que le cantaban y bailaban, porque Moctezuma era aficionado a placeres y cantares. Y aquéllos mandaba dar los relieves y jarros del cacao ... (*Historia* 323–4)

While he [Montezuma] ate, not even in thought could they make a racket, nor could the guards speak loudly in their own halls, near to that of Montezuma. They would take to him all of the fruits that could be found across the land, although he ate only a very little of it, from time to time. They brought in a certain drink made of cacao itself in fine gold cups; they said it was to facilitate relations with women, and so we did not look into it [his room], but what I saw was that they brought over fifty large jugs, made with good cacao, with its froth, and from that he drank, and the women would serve him with great compliance. And sometimes when it was time to eat there were some hunchbacked Indians, very ugly, because their bodies were small and fractured, and amongst one another they were vulgar, and other Indians were shameless, who gave thanks to him, and others, who would sing and dance to him, because Montezuma was fond of pleasures and songs. And to those he sent the leftover food and the jugs of cacao ... (Trans. RG & EC)

Likewise, in his *Relación de las cosas de Yucatán* (circa 1566), Diego de Landa associates beautiful women with the preparation and serving of chocolate, although his description does not go quite so far as Díaz del Castillo's assertion above that it would give "access" to women, stating only that "en estas fiestas les daban de beber mujeres hermosas las cuales, después de dado el vaso, volvían las espaldas al que lo tomaba hasta vaciado el vaso" ("at these parties they were served drinks by pretty women, who, after they handed over the cup, would turn their backs on whoever would drink from the cup until it was empty"; 84–5; trans. RG & EC). Rather, Landa focuses on the preparation, abundance, and taste, although the serving of the drink by women is consistent. While other accounts are not so favourable to the drink, Landa, like Durán, does seem to appreciate it for its flavour and refreshing nature: "Que hacen del maíz y cacao molido una manera de espuma muy sabrosa con que celebran sus fiestas y que sacan del cacao una grasa que parece mantequilla y que de esto y del maíz hacen otra bebida sabrosa y estimada; y que hacen otra bebida de la substancia del maíz molido así crudo, que es muy fresca y sabrosa" ("and they make out of maize and ground-up cacao a sort of foam that is quite flavourful, which they celebrate their parties with, and they extract from the cacao a sort of grease that resembles butter, and from this and maize they make another tasty and valued drink; and they make another drink from the substance of ground-up maize that is still raw, which is very fresh and tasty"; 82; trans. RG). Neither Landa nor Díaz del Castillo outright condemns the drink in his chronicles, but a letter thought to be attributable to the latter, likely written a few years after his *Historia verdadera* (1568), is more direct:

> La principal causa de su disminución, las vejaciones y molestias de algunos jueces allí proveídos, y también la codicia de los clérigos, y, todos ellos, por esta granjería de cacao. Andan tan distraídos algunos clérigos que no se acuerdan, en yendo a la visita del pueblo, de administrarles ni consolarles, sino [de] sacar sus libros de cuentas y deudas que les deben, y [de] hacer a los alguaciles del pueblo anden de casa en casa cobrando. (Qtd by Acuña 267–8)[7]

The main cause for the decline [of the province of Guatemala], the harassment and annoyance of some of the judges that were provided for, and the greed of the clergymen, and all of that, is the farming of cacao. Some clergymen are so distracted that they do not remember to visit the village, to administer to them or console them; rather they pull out their account books and the debts they owe them, and make the town sheriffs go around, charging house by house. (Trans. RG)

The debilitation that the use of chocolate causes religious figures is so intense, according to the letter, that the clerics forget to pronounce Mass. It is interesting that the charges of greed and neglect are raised against the clergy, made up primarily of Spanish missionaries, and not against the Indigenous peoples who provide chocolate or use it for their own purposes. Such vilification of chocolate as a problematic and distracting commodity can also be seen in how it is received by the religious community in Spain, as will be discussed in chapter 4.

All of the accounts of Cortés and his crew allude to the ceremonial nature of chocolate, both as a gift and as a part of celebrations. The missionary Juan de Torquemada notes in *Monarquía indiana* (originally published 1615) that cacao beans were also paid out by those who were fined for certain crimes: "Al que cometía fornicación, con viuda o esclava, condenabanle en sesenta plumas de las ricas, y preciadas, y otras veces en ciento, conforme era la culpa cometida; también se extendía esta condenación a otras cosas, como era Cacao, y Mantas" ("The man who committed fornication, whether it be with widow or slave, was fined seventy of the finest feathers, the valued ones, and sometimes [fined] by the hundred, depending on the committed fault; the condemnation was also extended to other things, such as cacao, and cloth"; 391; trans. RG & EC). Thus, the value of the cacao bean was high enough to fit the purposes of both gift and penalty.

In spite of the praise of the early conquistadors, many of the first Spaniards to try the drink were not entirely thrilled by the taste or preparation. Although Fray Acosta was a missionary who arrived far later than the first conquistadors, and whose *Historia natural y moral de las Indias* was not published until 1590, his perspective on the drink reflects that of earlier accounts. He recognizes the value the drink holds within Indigenous society and yet still believes it is an acquired taste that would not appeal to the uninitiated: "El principal beneficio de este cacao es un brebaje que hacen que llaman chocolate, que es cosa loca lo que en aquella tierra le precian y algunos que no están hechos a él les hace asco; porque tiene una espuma arriba y un borbollón como de heces, que cierto es menester mucho crédito para pasar con ello" ("The main benefit of this cacao is a concoction they make which they call chocolate, which is a crazy thing they value in that land, and many of those who are not familiar with it are repulsed by it; because it has a foam on top and a bubbling, resembling sediment, which is why it is necessary to give it much credit in order to get past it"; 180; trans. RG). He does, however, recognize that it has gained popularity among some Spaniards who have lived in the New World: "es la bebida preciada y con que convidan a los señores que vienen o pasan por su tierra, los indios y los españoles, y más las españolas hechas a la tierra, se mueren por el negro chocolate" ("the drink is highly valued and they offer it to the lords that come or go through their land, both Indians and the Spaniards, and even more so, Spanish women born here die for the dark chocolate"; 180; trans. RG & EC). That women, particularly, have displayed an intense fondness for the drink is somewhat prophetic of the reception it will receive on the other side of the Atlantic, and underlines the value that it has for both Indigenous and colonial communities. In spite of his own misgivings about the reception by those uninitiated in the taste, Acosta does mention that, although there are other, more beneficial goods, cacao is particularly well suited for transport "como es fruta seca, guardase sin dañarse largo tiempo, y traen navíos cargados de ella de la provincia de Guatemala" ("because it is a nut, it can be stored for a long time without it spoiling, and they bring loaded ships from the province of Guatemala"; 180; trans. RG). Its ability to be dried and transported for long periods of time makes it an ideal product for exportation to the Old World.

The passages which deal with the cultivation and creation of the drink attempt to relate the tree and its fruits in ways that the Spanish audience would understand. There were perhaps none more adept at this comparative knowledge creation than Gonzalo Fernández de Oviedo, whose writings and accompanying drawings helped to shape European understanding of the flora and fauna of the Americas for many years, even influencing the naming of many New World commodities. Although his full manuscript, *Historia general y natural de las Indias*, was not published until the mid-nineteenth century, there was a shortened version of the first part published in 1532, while the full version includes information on the conquest up to 1549. In his chapter dedicated to the cacao tree, he compares the leaves with that of the orange tree – a plant that would be much more familiar to his intended audience – and includes a drawing of the cacao leaf, in part because he acknowledges the audience's need to experience something visually, particularly an audience that otherwise would not have the opportunity to view the tree (268). Oviedo's intention is mainly to describe the physical objects that he finds, rather than go in depth into their uses or pre-Columbian histories, noting only that cacao can be used as a beverage or coin. The description is very much for an audience with no experience or access to the tree or its fruits, as he does not cover any of the more practical matters of cultivation, preparation, or consumption.

Motolinia, on the other hand, wrote a much more detailed explanation of the plant, its agronomy, and its uses:

> El cacao es una fruta de un árbol mediano, el cual lo plantan de su fruto que son unas almendras casi como las de Castilla, sino que lo bien granado es más grueso. En sembrándolo, ponen par de él otro árbol que crecen en alto y van haciendo sombra, y este árbol es como madre del cacao: da su fruta en unas mazorcas, señaladas sus tajadas

como pequeños melones. Comúnmente tiene cada mazorca de estas treinta granos o almendras de cacao, poco más o menos. Cómase verde, desde que comienzan a cuajar las almendras, que es sabroso, y también lo comen seco, y esto pocos granos y pocas veces; mas lo que generalmente de él se usa es para moneda, y corre por toda esta tierra. (84–5)

Cacao is a fruit from a medium-sized tree, which they plant from its fruits, which are something like almonds almost like the ones of Castile, but the seed is much thicker. In sowing it, they pair it next to another tree that grows tall and works as a shade; that tree is something like the mother of cacao. The cacao tree gives its fruit in cobs, each piece appearing like a little melon. Commonly each pod has thirty of these grains or cacao almonds, give or take. Eaten unripe, as soon as the almonds begin to take shape, it is tasty, and they also eat it dry, and this is with little grains and not often; more often than not it is used as currency, and it runs through all of the land. (Trans. RG)

Motolinia's description of the canopy of secondary trees protecting the cacao plant is echoed by Torquemada:

El cacao es una fruta de un árbol mediano, que el más alto no pasa de cinco varas, el cual lo plantan de su mismo fruto, en almácigos, y de allí lo trasponen como la oliva; (digo en el concierto por hileras, y calles muy concertadas) junto de él ponen una vara de otro árbol muy jugoso, que llama caccahuanantli, que quiere decir: madre del cacao; y es así, porque luego que se hinca la estaca, cobra vida, y se arraiga, y comienza a echar hoja, y a recibir la planta del cacao debajo de su sombra, con la cual le ampara de la fuerza del sol en el estío; y cuando ha menester calor, se la da, por estar sin hojas, la dicha madre, que es en el invierno; porque esta mata de cacao es de suyo muy delicada, y el mucho sol la ofende, y achucharra; y poco frio la hiela, por eso no se da, sino en tierras muy calientes, y se tiene mucho cuidado, con su beneficio, y cultura. (620)

Cacao is a fruit from a medium-sized tree, the tallest cannot surpass five yards, which is planted by its same fruit, in seed beds, and from there they transplant it like olives (I mean in ordered rows, and very well gathered lanes); next to it they place a stem of another tree that is very juicy that is called *caccahuanantli*, which means: mother of cacao; and it is just so, because after the stick is planted, it takes life, roots itself, and begins to grow leaves, and the cacao plant receives shadow, which shelters it from the strength of the sun in the summer; and when it needs heat, it is given so, by the mother, during winter; because this cacao plant in itself is very delicate, and lots of sun offends it, and it burns it; and little cold freezes it, which is why it is not found in lands unless they are very hot, and it must be taken care of, with its benefit and its culture. (Trans. RG & EC)

These passages give the uninitiated a much better understanding of the fruit, the tree it derives from, and the necessary agricultural conditions under which it can grow. There is little information regarding the taste or usage, other than Motolinia's assertion that it is sometimes employed as a currency. Generally, these works were sent back to Spain for the monarchs – or rather, their advisors – to gain some understanding of the new terrain over which they ruled, what economic benefits might be gained, and how to best continue their missions. Cacao did not seem to have many factors that would make it beneficial to the monarchy or its subjects at that time.

Although Motolinia does not go into great detail beyond the description of the plant itself, we find the first descriptions of the preparation of the drink in Acosta's text, which provides an overview of the different preparations and their potential medicinal properties:

Este sobredicho chocolate dicen que hacen en diversas formas y temples: caliente, y fresco y templado. Usan echarle especias y mucho chili; también le hacen en pasta, y dicen que es pectoral y para el estómago, y contra el catarro. Sea lo que mandaren, que en efecto los que no se han criado con esta opinión, no le apetecen. (180)

This aforementioned chocolate is said to be made in different forms and temperatures: hot, and cool and lukewarm. They tend to pour spices and a lot of chili in it; they also make it in a paste, and they say it is used as a remedy for the chest and stomach, and against colds. Whatever it may be, certainly those who have not been brought up with this opinion, do not crave it. (Trans. RG & EC)

Although brief, his description indicates that there are a variety of manners of preparation – hot, cool, and even in a paste – but with a focus on the potential health benefits, rather than enjoyment. Torquemada, on the other hand, indicates that there is a difference between the preferences of Indigenous and Spanish imbibers, with the Spaniards preferring a hot preparation, as opposed to the traditionally cold preparation of the Indigenous peoples (620). He also mentions the use of cacao beans as a monetary device, noting that a *xiquipil*, which consists of eight thousand beans, was worth between four and twelve pesos – depending on location and quality – at the beginning of the conquest; it had since then almost tripled in value in the century between the first encounter and the time he wrote *Monarquía Indiana*, first printed in Seville in 1615, after he had already returned to Spain. Although the bean never made it across the Atlantic as a form of currency, Torquemada does recognize that chocolate has gained a sort of value in Spanish society, in that the use of chocolate as a gift to those at home in Spain had already grown in popularity (620).

Bernardino de Sahagún, a Franciscan missionary during the first half of the sixteenth century, included a much more detailed explanation of the preparation of cacao in his *Historia general de las cosas de Nueva España*:

La que vende cacao hecho para beber, muélelo primero en este modo: que la primera vez quiebra o machuca las almendras; la segunda vez van un poco más molidas; la tercera y postrera vez muy molidas, mezclándose con granos de maíz cocidos y lavados; y así molidas y mezcladas, les echan agua en algún vaso. Si les echan poca, hacen lindo cacao, y si mucha, no hacen espuma. Y para hacerlo bien hecho se hace y se guarda lo siguiente, conviene a saber: que se cola; después de colado, se levanta para que chorree, y con esto se levanta la espuma y se echa aparte; y a las veces espésase demasiado; mézclase con agua después de molido. Y el que lo sabe hacer bien hecho, vende el cacao lindo, y tal que solos los señores lo beben, blando, espumoso, bermejo, colorado y puro sin mucha masa. A las veces le echan especies aromáticas, y aun miel de abejas, o alguna agua rosada. Y el cacao que no es bueno tiene mucha masa y mucha agua, y así no hace espuma, sino unos espumarajos. (717)

The one that sells cacao prepared as a drink grinds it first in this way: the first time she breaks or smashes the almonds [beans]; the second time they're to be ground a little more; the third and last time ground very finely, mixing it with boiled and washed grains of maize; and now that they're ground and mixed, the makers pour water in a cup. If they pour little, they make fine cacao, and if a lot, it doesn't foam. And to do it well, the following must be held to and done, which is: that it is to be filtered; after filtered, it is lifted and poured from a height, and with this the foam rises and it is separated; and when it becomes too thick, mix it with water after being ground. And he who knows how to make it well sells the fine cacao, and it is such that the lords drink, tender, foamy, auburn, dyed, and pure without much dough. At times they add aromatic spices, and even honey, or some rose water. And the bad cacao is that which has a lot of dough and a lot of water, and it does not form foam, only some bubbles. (Trans. RG & EC)

Although Sahagún focuses mainly on the proper procedure for making a pleasing beverage here, his analysis of how the drink is sold is reminiscent of the Nahuatl poem mentioned previously, "El vendedor de cacao." Good cacao makes good chocolate and will sell well and be drunk by nobility. Chocolate that comes out doughy is made from bad cacao, from the bad cacao seller who manipulates the beans to make them marketable, but ultimately makes an inferior drink, both in taste and spectacle.

Sahagún later turns his attention to the medicinal properties of chocolate as well. He suggests it as a part of a diet for those who are infected with "Trombiculidae" (known more commonly as chiggers) (738–9). He also suggests it as a cure for those who cough up blood (740) and those who are having trouble urinating (741). Still, it did not take long for the concerns regarding the potential side effects of the drink to appear in the writings of the missionaries and conquistadors, reflecting a debate that would continue in Spain in the following century. The account of the Anonymous Conqueror praises the drink, and is the first to assert its health benefits:

> Estas semillas, que llaman almendras o cacao, se muelen y se hacen polvo y se muelen también otras simientes pequeñas que tienen, y echan ese polvos en unos lebrillos que tienen un pico, después le echan agua y la mezclan con una cuchara, y después de haberlo mezclado muy bien lo cambian de un lebrillo a otro, de modo que haga espuma, la cual recogen en un vaso hecho a propósito; y cuando lo quieren beber, lo revuelven con unas cucharas pequeñas de oro o plata, o madera, y lo beben, y al beberlo se ha de abrir bien la boca, porque al ser espuma, es necesario hacerle sitio y que se vaya deshaciendo y pasando poco a poco. Esta bebida es la cosa más sana y de mayor sustancia de cuantos alimentos se comen y bebidas se beben en el mundo, porque aquel que bebe una taza de este licor, aunque se haga una jornada de camino, podrá pasarse todo el día sin comer otra cosa; y es mejor cuando hace calor que cuando hace frío, por ser de naturaleza fría. (113–15)

> These seeds which are called almonds or cacao they pound and reduce to powder, and also grind other small seeds and put the powder in certain jars with spouts. Directly they add water and stir with a spoon, and after it has been well beaten they pass it from one vase to another, which froths it, and this froth they collect in another jar kept for this purpose.

When they wish to drink it, they froth it with little spoons of gold or silver or of wood, and it is then drunk, but they have to open the mouth wide because it is froth, and must have room for liquefying little by little. This is the most healthful and most nutritious aliment of all known to the world, for one who takes a cup of it, though he may make a long journey, can pass all day without taking another thing, and being cold of its nature, it is better in hot weather than in cold. (Saville 41)

This begat the notion that those who drank chocolate would have enough energy to last them for a long time and through a variety of difficult tasks, a belief that would lead to contradictory religious decrees in Spain regarding chocolate as an acceptable beverage during times of fast.

Although the Anonymous Conqueror is unlikely to have been a medical practitioner,[8] there were indeed well-respected doctors who raised the question of the properties and benefits of chocolate, particularly on the Spanish constitution. The most prominent of those who were working in the New World is the doctor Juan de Cárdenas, whose *Problemas y secretos maravillosos de las Indias*, printed in Mexico in 1591, focused on the materials found in the New World and their potential medicinal effects. His two chapters on cacao and chocolate are longer than the others, which he himself recognizes and rationalizes given that he believes that the proper understanding and use of these products is the only way to avoid the complications that they could hold, particularly for those of Spanish descent (105v). This was a concern that was raised from the very beginnings of the conquest; as Rebecca Earle reminds us in the Introduction to *The Body of the Conquistador*, Columbus himself became convinced that without European foods, Europeans would not survive the climate of the New World (1–2). Cárdenas's main concern is with preparation, as he believes that it is improper preparation that can have a detrimental effect on the body:

... el cacao de su propia naturaleza sin tostarle ni prepararle con cosa alguna, tiene propiedad de restriñir el vientre, de detener de todo punto la regla, cerrar las vías de la orina, o pilar el hígado y mucho más el bazo, privar el rostro de su vivo y natural color, debilitar la digestión del estomago, acortar terriblemente el aliento con un molesto cansancio, causar paroxismos y desmayos, y a las mujeres sofocación o mal de madre, y sobre todo causa y engendra unas perpetuas ansias, y melancolías, y faltos de corazón que parece al que le ha comido que el alma se le sale, y al cabo habemos visto muchas personas, que le vienen a hinchar y dar en hidrópicos: y estos son los efectos que el cacao comido por si solo hace … (106r)

… cacao in its nature, without being toasted or prepared with anything, has the ability to stretch the belly, to stop everything, close the urinary tracks, destroy the liver and even more so the spleen, deprive the face of its lively and natural colour, weaken the stomach's digestion, terribly shorten breath with an unpleasant fatigue, cause paroxysms and fainting fits, and in women suffocation and nervousness, and above all it causes and procreates perpetual anxieties, and melancholies, and heart weakening so that it seems as if, whoever drinks it, their souls leave their bodies, and subsequently we have seen many people that come to inflate and have an insatiable thirst: and these are the effects that cacao has, eaten by itself … (Trans. RG)

Although Cárdenas's assessment of raw cacao would presumably discourage those who wish to try it, he quickly promises that the addition of other ingredients and proper cooking will actually counteract the same ailments he lists above:

Otrosí provoca la orina, es saludable remedio para toda opilación, ayuda a la digestión, despierta el apetito, socorre y repara los males de madre, causa alegría, y pone fuerza al cuerpo: que fuerte que podemos decir que si por una parte causa grandísimos daños, por otra vemos que los remedia tan de veras, que los convierte en contra de lo que de por si solo hacia de antes. Pidiese pues en el presente capítulo, que propiedades, o que misterio haya encerrado en esta pequeñuela fruta del cacao, para que della resulten tantos daños y provechos, y todos entre si tan contrarios. (106v)

Moreover, it provokes urination, it is a healthy remedy for any obstruction, it helps digestion, awakens appetite, it aids and heals nervousness, causes joy, and brings strength to the body: Surprisingly, we can say on the one hand that it causes great damage, on the other side we see that it works so well, that it turns against what it alone has previously caused. Therefore, we ask in the present chapter what properties or what mystery is enclosed in this little cacao fruit, so that from it results so much harm and benefits, and all among themselves so opposite. (Trans. RG)

Cárdenas devotes almost one-third of his book to the physical properties of Spaniards who are born or spend the majority of their lives in the Indies, arguing that the climate of the New World promotes changes that affect not only their physical being but also their overall quality of life. He is careful to note that these effects, particularly on the physical body, mean that those who spend a larger portion of time in the Indies may be more capable of withstanding the effects of its climate and produce. Cárdenas goes so far as to claim that the exposure of Spaniards to the Indies' climate both ages them more rapidly and potentially raises their IQs. Although the Indigenous peoples are also exposed to this climate, it affects them in different ways, according to his reasoning, since they already have the proper humours adapted to the humidity (Cárdenas 179v–180r and 183r–184v). As Earle demonstrates, it was food that was thought to balance the humours, and thus the differing foods – which, as we have seen, were so concerning to early conquistadors – also contributed to the vast external differences between Indigenous populations and Spanish settlers such as complexion, hair, and even visible ailments (*The Body of the Conquistador* 20–1).

In spite of the warnings of Cárdenas and others, chocolate quickly grew in popularity, particularly among the nobility, as will be discussed in future chapters. However, the question of the digestibility of chocolate by some constitutions is one that persists for some time. Although written almost a century later and on the other side of the Atlantic, Juan Francisco de Tejera's *entremés*, or inter-act play, *La rueda y los buñelos* (pre-1678)[9] links this concern to the old age of the protagonist, Vegete, as his maid prepares a feast for his fiancée:

ALDONZA. La lumbre encendía porque trate
   de hacerla cuando llegue el chocolate.
VEGETE. ¿Chocoqué?
ALDONZA. Chocolate.
VEGETE. Bueno, fuera,
   Que yo indigestas pócimas le diera
   A mi señora esposa, el día primero,
   Mejor regalo es el que hacerla espero. (167)

ALDONZA. The fire I lit so that I might have it ready for when the
   chocolate arrives.
VEGETE. Choco-what?
ALDONZA. Chocolate.
VEGETE. Well now, get out of here! That I should give undigestible
   potions to my dear wife on the first day, I hope to give a better gift to
   her. (Trans. RG & EC)

The servant, assuming that his – likely much younger – wife-to-be would have picked up the chocolate drinking custom of well-to-do ladies of Madrid, is ready to prepare the drink for her, while the protagonist – notably a "vegete," which the Real Academia Española defines as someone who is living a tranquil life, without work or other concerns, which is to say, someone who is likely older and retired – claims that it is too strong for his stomach, and would rather not give such a "present" to his future wife; instead he will make her "buñuelos" (hence the title), which are small fried balls of dough, a traditional sweet that he would be more familiar with, given his advanced age.

Still, in spite of all these potential issues, many of the early accounts laud the taste and effects of the drink. The earliest Spanish writings concerning the cacao bean and its properties are mainly concerned with the dissemination of knowledge, as opposed to later writings that will fictionalize its integration into Spanish society, a stance which only makes sense given the Spaniards' positions as conquistadors, missionaries, and official historians. Still, the conceptions of chocolate that appear in later Spanish literature are derived from these first accounts, from the potential medicinal properties to the aphrodisiacal qualities, and many of the original perceptions persist throughout the seventeenth century and well into the eighteenth.

CHAPTER 3

Chocolate-Covered Commerce: How Chocolate Came into Popularity in the Old World

The importation of goods from the Spanish American colonies presented the monarchy with a unique opportunity to expand its revenue from importation taxes. Unfortunately for the Spanish government, though the demand for goods such as chocolate, sugar, vanilla, and tobacco grew rapidly, it did not translate into a comparable increase in revenue. One reason that might be so can be found in the number of court cases and royal decrees in the period from the early 1600s to the mid-eighteenth century that demand payment from those who attempt to circumvent the law.[1] One such decree from 1634 states that any chocolate that comes "de fuera destos Reynos" ("from outside these kingdoms"), whether as a gift or for sale, will be taxed equally, and those who do not pay will be fined exponentially for each infraction (*Indice del acuerdo*). The need to lay out the exponential nature of the punishment indicates that there tended to be multiple infractions, often by the same perpetrators. Of course, chocolate had been tied to the potential for commerce even before the arrival of the conquistadors in what would become the Americas, with Indigenous groups using the beans as a form of currency. Thus, once it began making the transatlantic journey to Spain, chocolate could be expected to take on an important role in the economy of the Spanish Empire. Indeed, as we will see in the literary sources, chocolate, particularly that from the Oaxaca region, is used symbolically as a stand-in for value or worth, and the rapid decline in productivity from this region could also be read as nostalgia for a colonial past that was also rapidly disappearing. Janine Gasco points out that the Indigenous population of the Soconusco region dropped by over 90 per cent in the first fifty years of contact (389), likely taking with them the knowledge of cultivating cacao and producing traditional chocolate, in spite of its being what the Spaniards in the area saw as "their best opportunity to profit from the time spent in hot and unhealthy Soconusco" (390). By 1800, exports of cacao from this region dropped to five hundred *cargas*,[2] and the number of trees diminished by almost 75 per cent (390).[3]

The economics of a new good to be taxed and profited from – not to mention its relative scarcity in the early years – meant that, early on, chocolate tended to be a treat reserved for the nobility and wealthy. The first registers to mention chocolate identify very small amounts, likely only enough for personal use or gifts, as calculated by Marcy Norton, based on early shipments in 1595: "At a *very* conservative estimate of a small serving size of one ounce, twice a day, for a household of eight for a consumption of sixteen ounces a day, the fifty pounds would last fifty days" (296n, emphasis in the original).[4] Early court cases (*autos*) are of a civil nature, often involving the captain of a ship and two customers (or more) who had requested, been promised, and sometimes even prepaid for a small shipment of chocolate, only to find that the captain had sold it to someone else. A case in 1624, for example, brought by Guillén de Ayala and Francisco de Contreras against Juan del Castillo, the captain of the ship *El espiritú santo* (*The Holy Spirit*), demonstrates the rather limited amounts of chocolate that were being transported at that time. In the lawsuit, both de Ayala and de Contreras claim to have contracted Castillo to bring them each back two *cajones* (boxes) of chocolate, and that if he is unable to produce said boxes, he should pay 250 pesos in their stead, based on the estimated weight of more than 100 pounds. According to the captain's testimony, he had picked up four boxes, enough to satisfy both their demands, but, as is the way with transatlantic shipping, two had been lost to rough seas, and thus he could not fulfil both orders (*Autos entre partes* 1624). That two men would be willing to go to court for what appears to be a relatively small quantity speaks to the scarcity of chocolate in Spain at the time; nor is this the only case of its kind, particularly in the first half of the seventeenth century. The size of the boxes must have varied greatly, given that a decade later, in 1634, another case was brought forward by a priest, Fabián López, requesting 1,519 pesos – also possibly demonstrating a steep increase in the price of chocolate – in exchange for two missing boxes: "el uno dellos setenta cajas de chocolate de a dos libras cada una y el otro sesenta cajas de chocolate, así mismo de a dos libras" ("in one of them, seventy boxes of chocolate at two pounds apiece, and in the other sixty boxes of chocolate, also at two pounds apiece"; *Autos entre partes* 1634). This means that one box weighed 140 pounds and the other 120, while the earlier case only refers to the imprecise quantity of "more than" 100 pounds.

There are numerous similar cases that could be cited, but they are almost identical in complaint and result, save one that might help further the understanding of shipping weights of chocolate. In 1633, the treasurer of the Casa de la Contratación, the governing body that looked after all shipments made to and from the New World via Seville, brought a case forward against a ship's captain for having lost three *arrobas* of chocolate (*Autos entre partes* 1633). An *arroba* is a more precise measurement, defined in the *Diccionario de autoridades* as a weight equal to twenty-five pounds. Once again, the only justification given for being unable to produce the seventy-five pounds of chocolate is having lost it at sea. This particular case, however, does not help in determining the exact monetary value of chocolate, since the offending party is incarcerated, not fined.

In any case, the losses and lawsuits that arise during this period denote the difficulties of shipping goods across the Atlantic, particularly in the first part of the seventeenth century; but it is not only those who contract directly with shipping vessels who complain of difficulty procuring the drink. A letter written in 1627 by Diego de Aponte to his wife outlines the obstacles to finding chocolate in the Court, presumably at her request, given that it had been two years since any shipments had arrived from the New World (Aponte). His letter demonstrates that there is a shortage, while also indicating that there was at least some demand in Madrid, even in the first half of the seventeenth century. Given the shortage and resulting tension indicated by the letters and lawsuits of the 1620s and 1630s, María de Zayas's mention of abundant chocolate in her 1647 tome, *Desengaños amorosos* – particularly in contrast to its absence in her previous volume a decade earlier – further underscores that chocolate was much more available by the 1640s. This is not to say that there were no further cases after 1640, but the literary sources, at least, demonstrate that the commodity appeared to be more readily available in spite of any losses by individual importers. However, the increasing frequency of literary references to the drink, as well as the numerous lawsuits purporting chocolate's increasing value, do not directly demonstrate the actual value or economic benefits that it provided the crown, particularly, and perhaps paradoxically, as chocolate grew in popularity:

> The spread of material objects that occupied and stimulated the minds of consumers was flanked, on the one hand, by colonial groceries such as sugar, coffee, tea, cacao and tobacco and, on the other hand, by substances contributing to the bodily well-being through their dietetic or medical application such as cinchona or jalapa ... But a drastic reduction in their relative price made possible by an expansion of supply and improvements in product-specific transaction and transportation methods turned these goods into objects of mass consumption during the late-seventeenth and early-eighteenth centuries. (Fertig and Pfister 222)

Christine Fertig and Ulrich Pfister base their data primarily on tobacco and coffee, yet we can apply many of the connections regarding what they call the "glocalization" of goods to chocolate as well, as the spices and sweeteners used were greatly altered to suit local tastes once it reached European soil. Although Pamela Smith also focuses on the expanding consumption of goods in the early modern world, she believes that "Shared patterns of consumption emerged which placed great value on unique, rare, and unusual objects that could make real and tangible qualities of distant parts of the realm. The simultaneously social, moral, and exchange economy in which such wonders were embedded extended downward and outward through the courts of regional nobles" (48). Thus, chocolate was a good that rapidly went from being an exclusive, exotic novelty of the courts to a rapidly expanding, affordable product that was eventually accessible to the masses.

Still, the line from chocolate as representative of Other to status symbol for the noble class to general use product is not direct, which can be seen in the legal and historical documents of the period, as well as the literature. As has been discussed in previous chapters, the religious and medical debates may have caused some of this back and forth between acceptance and repulsion, but economic interests also played a significant role in the moral and social value of the commodity. Early literary sources dealing with commercial value place chocolate primarily in the New World, or, at most, in the hands of *indianos* – men who set out to win their fortunes in the Indies and who have since returned to Spain – vying for the undeserved attentions of Spanish noblewomen, underscoring a known trope in which returning conquistadors exploit their recent gains from New World exploration in order to supersede any supposed lack of familial fortune or good name.[5] Later, this Othering of chocolate is for comedic effect, relying on the similarity of *cacao*, a word with Indigenous origins, to scatological terminology in Spanish. As access to the drink became more commonplace, so too did the references to chocolate in a variety of settings, with a growing swath of character archetypes from all walks of life partaking. Still, even as it rapidly moved from status symbol to ubiquitous treat for all citizens, regardless of one's station in life, it maintained some of its mystique; accepted, even lauded, but still representative of the Otherness of the Indigenous world and peoples. This chapter will trace the move chocolate makes into various social settings, as well as the value placed on it within the literary and historical sources of Spain.

In Alonso Jerónimo de Salas Barbadillo's *El sagaz Estacio, marido examinado* (1620),[6] a play written in prose, the protagonists, Doña Marcela and Don Pedro, spar verbally over the virtues of different prototypical suitors that Doña Marcela is likely to encounter (and reject, as she has declared herself to be disinclined towards marriage). When Don Pedro suggests an *indiano* who has lost everything that he gained in the New World during the return trip to Spain, Marcela is intrigued, but still finds fault:

> Conténtame su persona, que a cualquier cosa se humillará un hombre que de las Indias viene pobre si aun los que vuelven ricos se valen de la mayor bajeza, como sea en defensa de su dinero: no obstante que esto del beber chocolate y tomar tabaco me desagrada, aunque lo segundo menos, porque es medicina con que se descarga la cabeza ... (Salas Barbadillo Acto primero)

> His person pleases me; if anything should humiliate a man, it is that he returns from the Indies poor, even though what makes them rich is the vilest of acts, whatever the justification of their money may be: all the same, this drinking of chocolate and taking of tobacco displeases me, although the second one less so, because it is a medicine that clears the head ... (Trans. RG & EC)

It is not his lack of money or status that bothers her, as, if she must marry, she would prefer a husband that she can mould to her own desires – which, as she tells Pedro early on in their dialogue, mainly consist of being left alone – but rather, she finds the drinking of chocolate and smoking of tobacco to be his most disgusting traits. Even then, chocolate appears to be the far worse offender. As such, the play connects chocolate directly back to the New World, and as a bad habit picked up by those who have been there, at that. Chocolate in this context is a symbol of Otherness, of undesirable qualities and/or peoples. *Indianos*, in spite of Marcela's assertion that a poor one would make a good husband because of his humility, would have been considered inferior suitors in general, even when they came back with all their new-found riches intact. This came from the belief that only men from poor or criminal backgrounds would risk the transatlantic journey to find new fortune, both economic and social. Men from good families with old money did not need to gamble with their lives or run away from their problems in order to gain access to marriageable women. Thus, chocolate being a habit of the *indiano* not only encapsulates its Otherness as a product of the Indigenous world but, in this early case, also labels it a low-class or criminal commodity, a marker of poor taste and overindulgence. Of course, Salas Barbadillo is well known for his satirization of daily life in Spain, particularly that of women who refuse to settle for anything less than perfection. Marcela's rejection of the *indiano* suitor simply because of his possible chocolate habit could be yet another of his satirical takes on the whims of women.

Another *comedia* to mention chocolate early on is Tirso de Molina's *Amazonas en las Indias* (1635). This *comedia* is part of a trilogy that Tirso wrote on the conquest of the Americas, following a trip he made to the New World. *Amazonas en las Indias*, set in the Amazon and following Gonzalo Pizarro's journey towards Peru, denotes a shift in the attitude towards chocolate within Spain, and yet still firmly places chocolate in the realm of the Other:

CARVAJAL. Los diablos y las mujeres
  dicen que sois de una casta,

  ...

  el diablo inventó a Guajaca,
  Guatemalas y Campeches,[7]

pues después que se conocen
en nuestra nación, se beben
en tres jícaras tres damas
cien escudos en dos meses. (3.2727–9, 2756–61)

CARVAJAL. They say that devils and women are part of one lineage ...
the devil invented Oaxaca, Guatemala, and Campeche, and since they
have been known in our nation, three women can drink a hundred
escudos in two months in three cups. (Trans. RG & EC)

According to Carvajal, one of the soldiers helping Pizarro conquer the
Incan empire, women in Spain have become so addicted to chocolate
that they drink it three times a day, and in two months spend one hundred *escudos* just on the drink. He maintains that the three best-known
production regions, as symbols for the drink, must have been invented by
the devil. This falls in closely with the well-accepted ideological understanding of the New World as the domain of the devil.[8] Yet, as Josefina
Sarabia Viejo and Isabel Arenas Frutos point out, by the eighteenth century even nuns were not immune to the siren song of chocolate; they
found that in a month's worth of food consumption at a convent in
New Spain, chocolate was only surpassed by meat and eggs, with vegetables coming in a distant fourth (260). Although it is difficult to know
exactly how much an *escudo* would have been worth, as it could refer
to a variety of different coins,[9] it is clear that Carvajal finds this to be an
excessive amount of money to spend on such a frivolous and potentially
dangerous habit. The fifteen-year difference in dates between *Amazonas*
and *El sagaz Estacio* shows that the attitudes towards chocolate were
beginning to shift on the peninsula, and yet – more than a century after
Cortés and his men witnessed Montezuma's chocolate ritual – it was still
considered a product of the New World and, particularly as described
here by Carvajal, a symbol of the devil's unchecked reign there.[10]

In spite of the decidedly negative connotations underlying Carvajal's tirade against both chocolate and women, the popularity of

the drink, according to *Amazonas en las Indias,* had skyrocketed among peninsular women in a short time. In spite of this, and later demonstrations of acceptance of the habit, it is worth noting that, during the second half of the seventeenth century and all the way up to the mid-eighteenth century, we still find reactions of disgust towards the product in literary sources. Even Pedro Calderón de la Barca, whose plays are often considered the culmination of baroque theatrical production and more highbrow than those by many of his predecessors, cannot resist making a scatological joke now and then. His *Gustos y disgustos son no más que imaginación* (1657) makes thinly veiled references to the homonymic nature of *cacao* and *caca.* The audience would have been well aware of the existence of chocolate, and thus would be in on the linguistic joke and understand that, while the sounds of *cacao*, with its Indigenous etymology, and *caca*, a somewhat infantile term for excrement in Spanish, might be similar, the words are not related in any way. In *Gustos y disgustos*, the *gracioso* (a servant who provides comic relief) is named Chocolate, which allows him to play with the double meaning of the word. Chocolate's master, Don Vicente de Fox, is in competition with the King for the woman he loves, and thus must sneak around, undetected. When the King finds Chocolate outside the woman's bedroom window, Chocolate must conceal his identity to protect that of Don Vicente, using wordplay to avoid the King's demand for his name:

> REY. Dime quien eres, o aquí
>   hoy a morir te resuelve.
> CHOC. Siempre que a escoger me dan;
>   lo mejor elijo siempre.
> REY. Pues muere, si es lo mejor
>   el ostentarte valiente.
> CHOC. El ostentarme gallinas
>   es muy mejor.

REY. ¿Pues quien eres?
CHOC. Un Chocolate, que ahora
    todo es ca-ca-o cuanto tiene. (26)

KING. Tell me who you are or resign yourself now to die today.
CHOC. Every time a choice is given to me, I always choose the best option.
KING. Then die, if it's best to flaunt your bravado.
CHOC. Flaunting myself as a chicken is much better.
KING. Then who are you?
CHOC. A Chocolate, that only has ca-ca-o now. (Trans. RG & EC)

While Chocolate desires to help his master, he is also a coward, and quickly gives in to the King's demand, naming himself a Chocolate, but one that is full of shit.

Calderón makes a similar reference in *La garapiña* (1678), when the main female character, Doña Blasa, is concerned that she is being left out. All of her other female friends have been afflicted with *flatos*, while she remains ignorant of their existence, as well as their meaning, as quickly becomes clear. In order to satisfy her desire, a suitor proclaims that he will procure them for her, when she refuses to hear his explanation of what they really are:

GALÁN. Advierte ...
BLASA. No hay que advierta.
    O flatos, o no entrar por esa puerta.
    Y en fin, para enmendar sus malos tratos,
    sor don Gil, o no verme, o traerme flatos. (Lines 78–81, emphasis in
    the original)

GALÁN. Listen ...
BLASA. There's no need for warnings. Either flatulence, or do not dare to
    darken this doorstep. That's it, to rectify your bad behaviour, Sir Gil,
    either you don't see me, or you bring me flatulence.

In order to disabuse her of her misunderstanding, he decides that he will bring her exactly what she desires and heads to the closest *botillería*[11] he can find. There he requests an odd mixture that leaves everyone else confused and repulsed:

GALÁN. ¿Tendrá usted a aquestas horas
   una garapiña helada
   de chocolate?
COQUERÓN. ¡E qué bona!
   De chocolat de Joan Jaca
   fato en Madrid por un negra
   que a puro sudar, le labra
   con tal forza, que le corre
   en pringa sobre la masa
   cuanto bebe.
GALÁN. Según eso,
   también tendrá limonadas.
COQUERÓN. ¡E piú belas! ... De agua e vin
   e de altras frígidas aquas
   sin auroras y sorbetes.
GALÁN. Pues mande usted que me vayan
   echando en esta redoma
   la garapiña, y de cuantas
   limonadas y bebidas
   tenga a estas horas en casa.
COQUERÓN. ¿Tuti junti?
GALÁN. Tuti junti.
COQUERÓN. ¡Oh, Dios mío!
GALÁN. ¿Qué se espanta?
COQUERÓN. De no trovar para qué es
   tan farfante mezcolanza. (Lines 104–25)

GALÁN. Do you happen to have a frozen chocolate drink?

COQUERÓN. And a very good one! The chocolate of Oaxaca made in Madrid by a black woman, who, by pure sweat, grinds it up so well that it saturates the dough of whoever drinks it.

GALÁN. Well then, surely you have lemonade as well.

COQUERÓN. And the best! ... of water and wine and of very cold waters without additives.[12]

GALÁN. Well, order them to start pouring the chocolate into this carafe, as well as any other lemonades and drinks you have currently.

COQUERÓN. All of it?

GALÁN. All of it.

COQUERÓN. Oh, my God!

GALÁN. What frightens you?

COQUERÓN. I dare not ask what this wicked hodgepodge is for. (Trans. RG & EC)

Money speaks, however, and the suitor promises to pay whatever the price is to secure his odd concoction, even though he admits to the audience in an aside that he does not have any means to do so. The shopkeeper Coquerón is satisfied and calls his helpers, the "Dona de las limonatas" and "Dona de las garapiñas." The latter arrives, wearing an outfit that announces her profession: "Sale la DAMA 1.ª con una túnica de lienzo hasta los pies, de color de chocolate, pintada de jícaras, con una en la mano" ("Out comes LADY 1. With a linen tunic all the way to her feet, the colour of chocolate, painted with jugs, with one in her hand"; line 142; trans. RG). The two Donas create the repugnant mixture with the help of a variety of other characters who toss in the ingredients they have on them, including a black man who claims to sweat red wine (line 151) and another woman who adds almond milk and cinnamon (lines 176–7). Once the drink is ready, Coquerón and Don Gil discuss the bill, fifty *reales* for the entire mélange, which Don Gil equates to "en plata / dos de a ocho" ("in silver, two pieces of eight"; lines 207–8).[13] He then pretends to have lost his coin purse, steals the drink, and runs back to the house of Doña Blasa, offering her the drink and all of the *flatos* that will accompany it: "Toma, Blasa de mi vida, / toma, y de flatos te hartas / hasta que revientes" ("Drink, Blasa, love of my life, drink it and you will be stuffed with flatulence until you burst"; lines 244–6; trans. RG & EC). The threat of gas-inducing chocolate is repeated in Francisco de Castro's interlude *Doña Parba Materia* (1702), but this time the woman in question is aware of the potential side-effect and refuses the offer (61).

In the much later, anonymous *Entremés del duelo del vejete* (1742), the linguistic connection between chocolate and excrement reappears, as we find one of the characters reluctantly receiving an offer of chocolate:

POLICRONIO Amigo, porque el susto no me mate,
    no me diréis, ¿cómo es el Chocolate?
DON ZYRILO. Es bebida, que dulce nos mantiene.
MATA. Y del Ca-cao, su bondad previene.
POLICRONIO. ¿Del Ca-cao? me asusto con oíllo;
    ¿y es regalo vuestro, o del chiquillo?
DON ZYRILO. ¡Ay, tal majadería! (83)

POLICRONIO. Friend, so that the shock does not kill me, won't you tell me, what is chocolate like?
DON ZYRILO. It's a drink, that keeps us sweet.
MATA. And its goodness comes from Ca-cao.
POLICRONIO. From Ca-cao? I'm scared just hearing about it; and is it a gift from you, or the little one?
DON ZYRILO. Oh, what nonsense! (Trans. RG & EC)

Although the short play was published in a compilation in 1742, it may have been written far earlier, which might make the character's ignorance of the drink slightly more understandable, but more likely this was done simply for the comedic effect. Here confusion resulting from the similarity between *cacao* and *caca* is being made all the more evident by Policronio's apparent distress over being asked to drink something made of *ca-cao*. There's no reason that the protagonists of either of these plays, particularly the latter, published in the mid-eighteenth century, would not have had access to, or at least knowledge of, chocolate, particularly if we look at the *décima* or "tenth" tax applied in the early half of the eighteenth century, as Nadia Fernández-de-Pinedo points out. According to her, foodstuffs account for 37.3 per cent of all privately imported goods that were taxed entering the capital from 1714 to 1743, with cacao and chocolate being surpassed only by sugar in total pounds imported per capita/per year (299).[14] Returning to the *entremés*, we could also read it as a criticism of Indigenous languages, which were seen as inferior and often ridiculed and eventually erased in favour of Spanish by conquistadors and missionaries alike. In any case, it appears that even the greatest literary minds cannot resist a good poop joke.

Although there is certainly some disdain for chocolate, mainly based on its Indigenous origins,[15] that persists throughout the colonial period and beyond, it also quickly converts itself into a status symbol. Francisco Santos's *Día y noche de Madrid* (1663) is a series of short dialogues which recount scenes of daily life in Madrid. Upon turning away from the life of the poor man, the narrator, Juanillo, tells his interlocutor, Onofre, about the rich man, whose life of leisure starts every day with his breakfast chocolate:

"¿Qué tiempo hace?" pregunta el poderoso por la mañana. Responde un criado: "Triste hace el día y está lloviendo." Bien responde este criado: triste y llorando está el día. Poderoso, abre los ojos del entendimiento y verás cómo cesa el tiempo de arrojar lágrimas para que lluevan tus ojos. Manda que cierren las ventanas y que le traigan chocolate. Vase levantando abriendo más boca que la tarasca. Salta de la cama y ya le espera un criado, ocupadas las manos con unas chancletas de terciopelo; pónselas en los pies y otro criado le echa en los hombros una capa de grana y pone en la cabeza una gorra de felpa. Siéntase cerca de la cama junto a un brasero de lumbre, no porque siente frío, pero basta el que ha oído decir que le hace. Vase calzando, entra el chocolate, tómalo y acábase de vestir. (660)

"What is the weather today?" asks the powerful man in the morning. A servant replies: "Sad is the day and it is raining." The servant responds well: sad and crying is the day. Powerful one, open your eyes to understanding and you will see how the climate ceases to give off tears so that your eyes may rain. He sends for the windows to be shut and to be brought chocolate. He gets up, his mouth opening wide as a chasm. He jumps out of bed and a servant waits for him, his hands occupied with velvet sandals to place on his feet, and another servant throws on his shoulders a dark red cape and puts on his head a plush hat. He sits near the bed next to a fire brazier, not because he is cold, but all it takes is for him to hear that it is cold outside. As he puts on his shoes, in comes the chocolate, he drinks it and finishes getting dressed. (Trans. RG & EC)

The rich man does not need to *feel* the cold to become uncomfortable, only to hear of inclement weather, and thus he must be consoled by luxurious goods meant to impart warmth, including the first hot chocolate of the day. Never mind that he is not actually cold, it suffices that his servants have felt that for him, and yet they are not included in the activities that bring comfort. It is Santos's *Día y noche* that also mentions the delicate nature of those who complain about chocolate, as discussed in chapter 4; so in spite of Juanillo's later assertion that chocolate has become a very common good in Spain (729), the only characters who partake of the drink are rich, delicate nobles.

Chocolate is also a way for young men previously unknown to Spanish society to demonstrate their status as newly rich *indianos*; even those who fail in their quest to bring back new-found wealth. In an early interlude, *Entremés famoso del calcetero indiano* (Diego de Govantes, 1646?), the title character is an *indiano* who has returned to Spain and become a "calcetero" ("hosier"), and whose main source of income comes from mending socks, "las peores que hallare" ("the worst that can be found"; 87).[16] In order to remind his neighbours of his status, even when poor, he mentions chocolate under seemingly illogical circumstances:

> GRACIOSO. ¿Qué hace, señor Olarte?
>   Parece, según se cae,
>   que ha comido chocolate.
> BÁRBARO. Bueno es el chasco, por Dios;
>   hemos de estar de levante
>   en casa de un caballero,
>   que hasta en Indias sé que saben,
>   ¿qué lo ganó por sus bríos
>   de la guerra en el combate? (92–3)

> GRACIOSO. What are you doing, señor Olarte? It would appear, given how you fall, that you have eaten chocolate.
> BÁRBERO. What a disappointment, my God, that we must stand on our feet in the house of a gentleman, who we all know has gone all the way to the Indies. What did your efforts in combat gain you over there?

The barber, who has been invited to sit down for a glass of wine, falls to the floor for lack of proper seating, and the titular character/owner of the house – named Gracioso to indicate the sarcastic or humorous tone of the interlude – claims that the barber must already be intoxicated on chocolate – a state not normally brought on by said drink – rather than admit that his house is in a too poor a state to host guests. The barber, however, brings our attention back to the house itself, and questions what happened to the supposed riches that gentlemen who have been to the Indies normally bring back with them. We can deduce, from the conflict that subsequently arises between Gracioso and his wife, that he has spent it extravagantly, and has thus wasted any fortune he might have gained earlier in life. The play ends with a song that reminds the barber to maintain his sobriety – "Lo que ahora le pido / al señor Olarte, / que no coma en su vida / más chocolate" ("I only ask that Señor Olarte never again eat chocolate in his lifetime"; 96) – but without a direct warning to those *indianos* who might lose their riches through lack of self-control.

In another interlude, *Entremés de la hidalguía* (1660) by Francisco de Monteser, the protagonist, Lorenzo, is a rich man who wants to marry a poor yet noble woman whose family has property that he can inherit, as well as a respectable name and lineage. Although Lorenzo himself is never identified directly as an *indiano*, he is certainly connected to them. When his cousin arrives to congratulate him on his upcoming nuptials, he promises to send the newlyweds half a dozen boxes of the good kind of chocolate, which he claims to drink every day for breakfast. When Lorenzo asks him if he has that much at home, he replies no, but that his brother will soon be making the transatlantic journey:

> y en pasando, es cosa clara
> que ha de casar ricamente,
> por ser de sangre tan alta,
> y me enviará a cuatro flotas
> diez cajones de comarca,
> y entonces os tomaré
> chocolate de importancia. (3)

> And in passing, it's a sure thing that he ought to marry richly, for being of such high status, he will send me, in four fleets, ten crates of the regional [chocolate] and then I will have chocolate of the highest quality for you. (Trans. RG & EC)

Lorenzo, aware of the ridiculous nature of his cousin's promise, given the amount of time and effort it would take to get that much chocolate across the Atlantic in time for his wedding, sarcastically replies "En aquel estado está / voy a calentar el agua" ("Well, if that's the state it is in, I'll put on the water"; 3).

Where Lorenzo's cousin is of noble blood, with the desire to marry rich, Lorenzo appears to be rich, with hopes of marrying someone of a good background to gain the status of old nobility. Both appear to be overly concerned with appearance over substance. Lorenzo's wealth seems to be new, which is reinforced later when he admits that he cannot read and must have his servant read a letter to him. The letter contains a request for a loan from a relative. Given his desire to marry someone with property and a name in Spain, his connection to family in the Indies, his apparent illiteracy, and the requests for money from his family, Lorenzo should be considered an *indiano*, even though he is never explicitly named as one. Chocolate is brought up once again at the end of the play when his would-be bride arrives and grills him on the status of his fortune. When he cannot produce any of the goods she requests, especially since any chocolate he might own is still in Oaxaca – which would make it rare chocolate of a high quality, albeit on a different continent – she despairs, and they call off the wedding. Without the chocolate that symbolizes his New World wealth, she has no reason to marry someone otherwise so far below her station.

Only a year later, Agustín Moreto's *No puede ser el guardar una mujer* (1661) presents chocolate as both a status symbol and a commonplace good – at least for the upper classes. Moreto himself is associated with at least five plays or interludes that reference chocolate frequently, demonstrating that he considered it an important enough cultural touchstone to include it in a significant portion of his oeuvre. When the *gracioso* of this play, Tarugo, pretends to be an *indiano* named Don Chrisanto to gain access to a nobleman's house,[17] he claims that the boxes he brings with him are filled with fragile contents that prove his status:

PEDRO. ¿Pues qué es lo que viene en ellas?

TARUGO. Chocolate de Guajaca,
   y filigranas diversas,
   jícaras de Mechoacán
   y paños que dar con ellas. (18)

PEDRO. Well, what is in them?

TARUGO. Chocolate from Oaxaca, and many filigrees, *jícaras* from
   Michoacán, and cloth to go along with them. (Trans. RG)

That he names the chocolate from Oaxaca before the jewellery, decorated jars, and cloth denotes the special status and value he places on it. This could, in part, be attributed to his status as a *gracioso* and servant; it would be unsurprising to find either of those character archetypes thinking about food first and everything else later.

In spite of this preliminary allusion to the valuable nature of chocolate in the play, later commentary reveals a more nonchalant attitude towards the drink. When Tarugo, still posing as a visiting *indiano*, has a guest (his actual master) arrive at Don Pedro's house, he requests that chocolate be prepared for them, as it is "el preciso agasajo, / que a una visita se debe" ("a precious warm welcome, the debt owed to a visitor"; 24). However, when the chocolate finally arrives, his guest, Don Félix, is reluctant to partake, as it would be the third time that day that he has been offered the drink:

FÉLIX. Señor,
   eso por mí es escusado
   que le he tomado dos veces.

TARUGO. No se os dé nada, tomadlo,
   que el chocolate en Madrid
   se usa ya como el tabaco. (26)

FELIX. Sir, please excuse me from it, as I've already drunk it twice.

TARUGO. Do not worry about it, drink it, chocolate in Madrid is now used like tobacco. (Trans. RG & EC)

Félix's reluctance to drink chocolate for a third time, along with Tarugo's assertion that it is as widespread as tobacco, points to the commonality and even overabundance of chocolate in Spanish society by the mid-seventeenth century.[18] Although Felix is eventually convinced by Tarugo and their host, Don Pedro, to accept their hospitality, he is not nearly as impressed as Tarugo, who normally would not be invited to participate in such entertainments. Tarugo's overenthusiastic imbibing of the chocolate becomes quite the spectacle for their host, since he is unaware of Tarugo's real status as Felix's servant:

TARUGO. Cuerpo de Dios, ¡qué bien hecho!

PEDRO. Mucho toma el Don Chrisanto. *Ap.*

FÉLIX. Si es deuda de cortesano,
    para cumplimento basta.

TARUGO. Dadlo acá si dejáis algo. (24)

TARUGO. Body of Christ! well done!

PEDRO. Don Chrisanto drinks quite a lot. (*Aside*)

FELIX. If it is debt of the courtier, he is paid up.

TARUGO. Give it here, if you have some left. (Trans. RG & EC)

Not only does he gulp down his own so quickly as to provoke a reaction in his host, he also requests that they leave their leftovers, which reminds the audience of his true nature, as servants often only got to eat the remnants of their master's meal. Don Pedro, in spite of his initial reaction to Tarugo/Don Chrisanto's gluttonous ways, appears to overlook this detail, but his reaction demonstrates that for the upper middle and noble classes, drinking chocolate would be a normal daily interaction, and not one that would normally provoke such an exuberant response. The use of chocolate as a symbol, therefore, in *No puede ser el guardar una mujer* is left somewhere between its ability to denote status and an increasing general use, at least among upper-class citizens. Tarugo's gleeful reception of the chocolate belies the idea that it could be so widespread yet as to be a part of even servant life.[19]

No puede ser coincides with a number of mid-seventeenth-century complaints that chocolate was being brought into Spain outside of the normal channels of trade. In 1663, just two years after *No puede ser*'s publication, the King himself wrote about the flagrant disregard for his orders, thus prohibiting the importation of any chocolate outside of his jurisdiction:

Por cuanto se ha entendido, que de algún tiempo a esta parte se han introducido por los puertos destos mis Reinos muchas cantidades de cacao fuera de registro, en contravención de mis Reales ordenes, por las cuales está dispuesto, que no se puedan traer ningunos de los frutos de mis Indias Occidentales debajo de ningún pretexto, sino es en mis Flotas, y Galeones de la Carrera de Indias, o en los Navíos, que con registro, y licencia mía van a ellas. Y no habiendo motivo que obligue a tolerar los excesos que se comenten en comerciarse por otra vía, en contravención de mis Reales ordenes; he resuelto, que todo el cacao, y demás géneros de las Indias, que se trajeren a los puertos, o demás Lugares destos mis Reinos por vasallos míos, o otras cualesquier personas, no habiendo venido en mis Flotas, y Galeones, o Navíos de registro, se aprehendan, y den por perdidos, como cosa ilícita, y prohibida. (Domingo Víctor de la Cruz 22r)

For as much as it has been understood, up to this point, that there has been introduced, through the ports of this my kingdom, a vast amount of unregistered cacao, in direct contravention of my royal orders, it has been decreed that no produce from my occidental Indies can be brought under any pretext, unless brought by my fleet, and by galleons of the

Indian route, or in the vessels that are registered and with my licence go to them. And I find no reason that obliges me to tolerate the excess that is talked about in dealings by another route, as a contravention of my royal decrees; I have decided that all cacao, and other produce from the Indies, that have been brought to the ports or other places within my kingdom by my vassals, or any other people, not having come in my fleet, and galleons, or vessels that are registered, shall be given up as lost, as illicit things, and prohibited. (Trans. RG & EC)

While not direct evidence of widespread trade, this demonstrates that enough chocolate is being brought to Spain for the King to wish to take total control. It is obvious that at this point chocolate is a valuable and frequently imported commodity, meaning that a large number of people were partaking and willing to pay for it, whether it was brought to Spain by legal means or not.

Another mid-seventeenth-century play, *La fregona* (1655), presumed to be written by Juan de Matos Fragoso,[20] also denotes the overuse of chocolate by having a character refuse a serving, but this time it is a woman, Casilda, who rejects the offering: "Que ya me enfada tanto chocolate, / a esta moza lo dad, que de estas cosas / siempre son las criadas más golosas" ("So much chocolate irritates me, give it to the servant girl, it is always the help that are the most gluttonous for these sorts of things"; 13; trans. RG & EC). This rejection of chocolate by a woman is almost unheard of in any of the other literature or treatises of the period, but, as Amado Doblas points out, it is all part of an elaborate ruse on the part of the protagonist to create the illusion of wealth and high social status ("En el V centenario I" 276). These few lines also demonstrate that, while the servant class might enjoy sweets, they would still have less access to them. Likewise, Calderón de la Barca's *El pésame de la viuda* (1651), written only a few years earlier, also has a female character reject chocolate, not because she is sick of it, but because she believes that her status as a widow prohibits her from imbibing:

¡Qué porfiada
estás! Anda, Isabelilla,
chocolate no me traigas
ni por pienso, que es regalo,
y a mí no me hacen falta.
Unos huevos y torreznos
haz que para una cuitada,
triste, mísera viuda,
huevos y torreznos bastan,
que son *duelos y quebrantos*. (Lines 62–71, emphasis mine)

You're so stubborn! Go on, Isabelilla, don't bring me chocolate, I can't even think about it, as it is a gift, and I don't need it. Just make some eggs and bacon for this shy, sad, and miserable widow, eggs and bacon will suffice, since they are *wounds and suffering*.

The widow, rather than showing off her status, is trying to make the whole world know her suffering and suffer with her. The phrase "duelos y quebrantos" can be literally translated, as I have done here, as "wounds and suffering," but is also the name of a well-known dish in Spain, which the Quixote himself also eats often, and is similar to what she has already asked for, scrambled eggs and bacon or chorizo.

There would appear to be a rather large gap between the early literary sources, which show either disdain or disinterest in chocolate as a commercial good in Spain in the 1620s and 1630s, and the acceptance and widespread dissemination of its use among all classes in the second half of the seventeenth century. The historical documents in the Archivo de las Indias in Seville, the period from the publication of Tirso de Molina's *Amazonas* (1635) to Calderón's *Gustos y disgustos* (1657), are rife with examples of smuggled goods, including, in many cases, chocolate that has come to Spain outside of the normal customs process. Although this does not explain the lack of literary sources that allude to the economic value of chocolate during the twenty-some middle years of the 1600s, it does give more context to the King's decree above.[21]

Chocolate is indeed, by the mid- to late seventeenth century, at least ubiquitous enough for Calderón to include it in a list of debts owed. In his *entremés* titled *La rabia*,[22] a noblewoman is besieged by purveyors asking her to pay off her debts to them for various goods. One, an African, requires payment for three boxes of good chocolate. When she cannot produce enough money to pay off all of the bills, the various vendors fight for first rights, with the African proclaiming "Primero son mis guajacas" ("First comes my Oaxacas"), to which she replies, "Primero es que el diablo a todos / lleve" ("First is that the devil may take them"; *Entremés de la rabia* lines 218–20; trans. RG & EC). The short play ends with all of the debts unpaid and each of the vendors proclaiming his *rabia*: "NEGRO. Yo, que aunque venga la flota, / lo mismo el cacao se valga" ("NEGRO. For me, though the fleet may come in, the cacao is worth the same"; lines 345–6; trans. RG). Although there is no indication of why Doña Aldonza has to have so much chocolate in her house, it, along with her other debts, suggests a life of appearances. She has the chocolate most likely for the same reasons presented in *No puede ser* and Olmedo's *Las locas caseras* (1708), which is to say, for hosting purposes. Her other debts, to a tailor and a Frenchman for the elaborate outfits and jewellery they have provided her, make it seem as though she has gone to great lengths to keep up an exterior show of wealth. Of course, she has a gossipy neighbour visiting while her creditors come one by one to the door with hands outstretched, which is probably far more damaging to her reputation than if she had been without chocolate or the latest fashions once in a while. The willingness to go into debt, in the case of Doña Aldonza here – or to mix the trace amounts of good chocolate left in the house with whatever else is available, in the case of María in *Las locas caseras*, as will be discussed below – testifies to the false nature of early modern Spanish society. Chocolate is just one more way in which the noble classes can hide their defects from their guests, but in the end their riches and good graces are nothing more than thinly veiled lies. In both cases, however, the lie comes back to haunt them, in the former case in the form of a gossipy neighbour who learns the truth, while in the latter, the hostess and her guests are literally stained by it, when the servant, Barbulilla, trips and spills hot chocolate on everyone (Olmedo 88).

The connection to debts and demonstration of wealth in these plays is an interesting one, and one that reflects court cases of the day. Among the many *autos* of individuals proclaiming their ownership based on promises and pre-payments of chocolate being brought back by ship captains, we find the 1676 case of María Josefa Ortiz, the wife of one Francisco Hernández of Seville, who wishes to be granted ownership over the chocolate her husband has ordered, in lieu of the return of her dowry upon their separation:

> ... digo que me hallo separada del dicho mi marido en virtud de autos que se han seguido ante el eclesiástico y esto y siguiendo sobre la restitución de mi dote ante la justicia real desta ciudad, por cuya dependencia se han embargado los bienes que poseíamos para apreciarlos y liquidar lo que valen, y respecto de no alcanzar a mi dote las otras y atento a que es llegado a mi noticia que en el navío Jesús Nazareno nuestra señora de la soledad de que es maestre don José Castaño y vino en compañía de la presente flota con registro de la Provincia de Caracas ... trae el dicho mi marido algunas partidas de cacao y para que conste las que son y se pueda hacer el cuerpo de bienes por entero de forma que yo no quedé ocultándolas con perdida de mi dote. (*Autos entre partes de 1676*)

I say that I find myself separated from my said husband in virtue of the petitions that have been sent before both the ecclesiastical court and this one and following the restitution of my dowry before the royal justice of this city, on whose authority we had to value and sell off the goods we possessed for their actual value, which have been seized, and because I

have no access to my dowry, it has come to my attention that in the ship
Jesus Nazareno Our Lady of Solitude, whose grand master is Don Jose
Castaño, who came in company of the present fleet with registry from
the province of Caracas ... my aforementioned husband thus brings
some shipments of cacao, and thus it must be figured out how much
they are [worth] and then we can have an idea of the whole body of
goods so that they cannot be kept hidden with the losing of my dowry.

Chocolate is considered valuable enough to replace her lost dowry, which
she feels her husband owes back to her upon their separation. The manner in which she explains her separation, "que me hallo separada del
dicho mi marido," makes it sound as if it was something done *to* her, and
not of her own volition, and she puts it this way because she wants and
likely needs to recuperate her dowry, particularly as divorce and remar-
riage were unlikely under the tenets of the Catholic Church at the time.

The economic value and scarcity of good chocolate are echoed in
the interludes *El figurón* (1702) by Francisco de Castro and *Las locas
caseras* (1708) by Alonso de Olmedo. Castro's reference is more subtle
than Olmedo's: the protagonist questions the preparation of chocolate
that claims to be from Oaxaca:

FIGURÓN. Decid, ¿me la habrán hecho con Guajaca?
PAJE 2. Con Guajaca está hecho, ¿quién lo niega?
FIGURÓN. Más parece que está con jirapliega,
    porque por Cristo que la espuma sabe
    a purga con su punta de jarabe:
    fuego de Dios. Sacad.
    Arrójalo (Entremés del figurón 4)

FIGURÓN. Say, did they make it for me with Oaxaca?
PAJE 2. With Oaxaca it is made, who can deny it?
FIGURÓN. It seems more like a laxative, because, by Christ, just tasting
    the foam will purge with its syrup: fury of God. Get rid of it! *Throws
    it.* (Trans. RG & EC)

The Figurón is so well versed in the composition and taste of various chocolates that he is convinced that someone is trying to pass off an inferior product and is so disgusted by it that he throws it away. While not explicit in its condemnation of such practices, or the reasons why there may be a need to mask the quality of the product, this scene from *El figurón* does demonstrate that the origin of the bean had come to have meaning in Spanish society. The use of the word "figurón" to refer to the protagonist also indicates a criticism of this practice, as a "figurón" is someone who worries about appearing rich or noble while, in fact, being neither (*Diccionario de autoridades*).

Olmedo's version is much more direct in remarking on the scarcity of quality chocolate: "MARÍA. ¿Quedó algún chocolate de Guajaca? / BARBULILLA. Un poquito quedó allí, que es cosa escasa. / MARÍA. Revolverásle con el que hay en casa" ("MARÍA. Was any of the chocolate from Oaxaca left over? BARBULILLA. There's a bit left, but very little. MARÍA. Mix it with what's left at home"; *Entremés de las locas caseras* 81; trans. RG). Although this interlude is most likely from an earlier date,[23] it shows the difficulty of getting, and keeping, good chocolate – whether because of shipping issues or personal economic troubles – which was so necessary to demonstrate that one was a good hostess. In fact, when the chocolate is later destroyed by a servant who trips over a dancing boy, causing her to splatter chocolate all over María and her guests, María's first concern is the ruined chocolate, only then followed by the health of her child.

The quality of the chocolate drink also affected its value. While María of *Las locas caseras* mixes the Oaxaca chocolate with whatever other cacao she has at home, the titular characters of *Las beatas* (1664), an interlude by Antonio Barrientos, know that the chocolate they are able to purchase at a discounted price is less than ideal, but they'll drink it anyway:

MUJER 2. Lindo chocolate tengo
   que un criado de un Marqués
   me le vendió.

MUJER 1. ¿Y era bueno?

MUJER 2. A seis reales me costó,
   que de regalo lo han hecho
   con muchas cosas cordiales,
   y siempre que lo bebo
   con los terrones tan gordos
   de piedra bezal encuentro. (*Mojiganga de las beatas* 22)

WOMAN 2. Sweet chocolate I have, that a servant of a marquis sold
   to me.

WOMAN 1. And was it good?

WOMAN 2. It cost me six *reales*, they practically gifted it to me, with
   many cordial things, and every time I drink it I find such big lumps
   of bezoar stone. (Trans. RG & EC)

Although we do not know how much chocolate they have, it appears that the six *reales* they paid for it is considered so low a price that it was practically free. The inclusion of bezoar in the drink might indicate that it is of such low quality that it might be detrimental to their health.[24] It certainly does not seem like the most precious gift in any case, since it is so difficult to drink that another character responds, "Este es chocolate, que / se come, y se bebe a un tiempo" ("This is chocolate, that is eaten and drunk at the same time"; 22; trans. RG), referring to the incredible viscosity of the supposed "drink."

Chocolate – at least good chocolate – is still portrayed as something of a status symbol; its pervasive presence, particularly in *entremeses*, those inter-act plays that often take everyday occurrences to their extreme for comedic effect, demonstrates its widespread reception in Spanish society, from the lowest to highest echelons. One in particular, the *Mojiganga de los niños de la Rollona y lo que pasa en las calles* by Simón Aguado (date unknown),[25] directly mentions a *barrendero* (street-sweeper) as a consumer of chocolate:

HOMBRE. ¿Has almorzado, Domingo?

BARRENDERO. Sí, chocolate me dieron

   en la Cava, y los biscochos

   me parecieron muy torreznos,

   porque estaban muy salados.

MUJER. Yo los comí por eso.

   Holgárame de saber

   si el chocolate midieron

   por cuartillos.

BARRENDERO. Por cuartillos

   es todo lo que yo bebo. (*Los niños de la Rollona* lines 285–94)

MAN. Have you eaten, Domingo?

BARRENDERO. Yes, they gave me chocolate at the cellar, and the biscuits

   looked like rashers of bacon, they were so salty.

WOMAN. That's why I ate them. I find pleasure in knowing if they

   measured the chocolate in quartiles.

BARRENDERO. By quartiles is all that I drink. (Trans. RG & EC)

Both this and other statements made by and about the *barrendero* point to the street-sweeper being a drunk, and thus it is difficult to be sure whether his drink was purely chocolate or something else entirely. Still, the representation of someone as lowly as Domingo having access to chocolate points to the possibility that it is no longer solely a commodity for the rich and noble classes of Madrid. The *entremeses*, however, were also known for their ironic and satirical take on life, with little respect for the unities that bind three-act plays, making them difficult to interpret. The drinking of chocolate and overindulgence by the lower class could be a stand-in for social critiques of more important people, particularly since the term *barrendero* was applied primarily to those who worked in churches, convents, and palaces, not to streetsweepers (*Diccionario de autoridades*).

Although it will be discussed further in a later chapter for its merits in the medical debates on chocolate, it is worth looking at the 1669 recommendation on commerce and tariffs made to Mariana de Austria as regent to King Carlos II, which states that it is nearly impossible for the customs officials in Seville to keep up with the amount of merchandise coming in, not only from legitimate but also illegitimate sources, and that forcing another tax will only hurt the citizens of Spain, not the merchants. Chocolate is mentioned as a nutrient that has become so necessary that even the lowest of people will be ill affected by any further imposition or taxation on it (López and Pérez de Herrera 172–173v). Not only will the health and well-being of all citizens be affected, the letter continues, but the merchants will create a black market to circumvent any extra costs: "Demás de la alteración general de los precios se ha de ocasionar al comercio gran daño, y confusión, y a los comerciantes muchas vejaciones, y molestias, y estos indubitablemente han de hacer fraudes" ("Aside from the general alteration of prices, great damage to business will be caused, and confusion, and to the traders many annoyances, and troubles, and they will undoubtedly commit fraud"; 174r; trans. RG). According to the councillors of Madrid, this is the inevitable result of any newly imposed tax, and thus to benefit the citizens of Spain, and avoid the complications of illegal trade, they recommend abandoning the efforts to control trade that, thus far, have been unsuccessful.

Perhaps the most damning representation of the social expectations surrounding chocolate and hospitality are in Ramón de la Cruz's short play *Las tertulias de Madrid o El porqué de las tertulias* (1770). De la Cruz (1731–1794) was writing some one hundred years later than Calderón, when chocolate had been even further ensconced in Spanish society, and his *Tertulias* provides a biting, satirical look at the state of the Spanish court in the late eighteenth century. As a clerk in the ministry of finance, he was likely not from the highest echelons of society and yet probably had access to or at least a view of their daily lives – and more importantly, their expenses. The *tertulias* of Madrid were similar to the salons of French society, where upper-class women hosted intellectual gatherings to discuss the politics and culture of the day. In this *tertulia*, however, the guests are all rude and demanding. Upon arriving, they are informed that their host, Doña Inés, is unavailable because her husband has fallen gravely ill and she is in search of an emergency physician. Rather than excusing themselves quietly to allow for Inés to attend to her ailing husband, they insist on staying. They demand food and drink, sing loud, raucous songs, and go so far as to request lodging for the night, while Inés runs back and forth, discussing her husband's condition with doctors and crying visibly. Of the demands they make, chocolate is the first, as they have become accustomed to its presence in any event (see image 3.1):

DOÑA LAURA. Hija, en estos lances y entre
    personas de confianza,
    no te andes con chocolate,
    meriendas ni pataratas,
    lo primero es lo primero
    que se ha de cuidar; y basta
    con que saquen una fuente
    de fruta, alguna fritada
    o torreznos.
DOÑA FRANCISCA ¿Tienes lomo
    fresco?
DOÑA INÉS Voy a que lo hagan freír.
    (*Se levanta.*)
DOÑA ANA. A mí, chocolate;
    que hoy estoy desazonada.
DOÑA JUANA. Yo, mi media rosca tierna
    y mi puñado de pasas,
    como siempre.
DOÑA FRANCISCA (Aparte.) ¿Habrá mujeres
    más imprudentes? (Lines 211–26)

DOÑA LAURA. Daughter, in these predicaments and with people we trust, do not go along with chocolate, snacks, or silly things; the first of these is what you should watch more closely, and it suffices if they just put out a fruit fountain, some fried food or slices of bacon.
DOÑA FRANCISCA. Do you have fresh loin?
DOÑA INÉS. I'm going to get them to fry it. (*Getting up*)
DOÑA ANA. For me, chocolate; for I'm quite irritated.
DOÑA JUANA. For me, my half of soft rosca[26] and my handful of raisins, as always.
DOÑA FRANCISCA. (*Aside.*) Could there be more imprudent women?
(Trans. RG & EC)

In spite of Doña Francisca's somewhat self-aware statement, she is still the one that demands fresh pork loin to be fried up. Later, when they ask to stay the night and Inés balks at the request, saying that she does not have enough room for them all, or enough food to feed them all dinner, they proclaim that with a bit of ham, some coffee, and chocolate, they'll be just fine (lines 455–64). Of course, all of the undesirable guests at this unwanted party are happy to take advantage of Inés's hospitality and unfortunate situation, but when presented with the prospect of having to host someone themselves, they all have quick and convenient excuses. Don Juan, Inés's indisposed husband, eventually recovers and arrives to break up the party. He has apparently never thought that the *tertulias* that his wife hosts are worthy of her efforts and picks apart each guest's faults, accusing them of only attending for their own gain and not to participate in the intellectual exchange that Inés desires. In doing so, he not only rids himself of the meddlesome and greedy guests but also cures his wife of her fixation on *tertulias* and the not-so-intellectual life of Madrid. De la Cruz's satirical representation of Madrid's social life in the second half of the eighteenth century is equally critical of the participants and its rituals and requirements, such as the providing of chocolate to any guest, wanted or otherwise, who shows up at your door.

Figure 3.1 *La xocolatada* Barcelona, 1710. Courtesy of Museu del Disseny, Barcelona. This image, made up of tile plates, depicts a party where the main theme is chocolate.

Still, the increasing popularity of chocolate cannot be denied. Even by 1682, almost one hundred years before de la Cruz's *Tertulias*, it is considered so important to the social and even medical well-being of Spanish citizens that the King declares that it should be allowed in tax free (Fernández de Madrigal 222v). Of course, this would be Carlos II, who was well known for his excessive love of chocolate,[27] and thus the decree might be read through the lens of his own desire to make chocolate more accessible. This decree was not without its detractors, with some of the King's own councillors reminding him that the revenue loss would be potentially detrimental:

> Una carta de siete deste mes refiere Vm que por la representación que sacia el consulado se reconocería la inteligencia que sea dado a la cédula de veinte y seis de octubre deste año en que se declara ser libres en la entrada el cacao chocolate azucares vainillas y achiote, pero que en los derechos de millones por lo que toca a el consumo ... que el consulado refiere siendo tan gravoso que tiene con desasosiego a todos los comerciantes de Indias y que siempre que los jueces sean públicos sea movido entre discordia causando inquietud e instancias al consulado ... (Fernández de Madrigal 222v–223)

> In a letter of the seventh of this month Your Majesty refers to the representation that satiates the consulate and would acknowledge the attention that should be given to the decree of the twenty-sixth of October of this year, in which it is declared that free entry of cacao, chocolate, sugars, vanillas, and achiote, but for the rights of millions [taxes] which comes into play for consumption ... to which the consulate refers as being so burdensome that it has every trader of the Indies feeling uneasy and that as long as judges are public, will be moved to discord, causing worry and petitions to the consulate ... (Trans. RG & EC)

In spite of these warnings, foreign ships continued to traffic in illicit goods, which caused the Fiscal Council of Seville to request that all non-Spanish ships be banned from bringing in "cacao ni otros géneros de Indias" ("cacao or other goods from the Indies"; *Autos fiscales*). This debate regarding who could import chocolate and whether or not they would pay for the privilege continues for several decades, long after the decrepit Carlos II passed away heirless at the end of the seventeenth century. Shortages in the early part of the eighteenth century allowed for the French to trade more freely with Spain, in spite of a long-standing rivalry (*Papeles Varios* 170v). Still, such ideas were met with vehement dissent, in this particular case for the following reasons:

> El primero de que es contra las leyes, y cédulas reales no necesita de más justificación que la lectura de los libros y cuadernos en que por órdenes reales están recopiladas e impresas ... El segundo de que se perjudica a los reales intereses, y a los vasallos, tampoco necesitaría mucha explicación si en España fuese más común el conocimiento de las reglas, y de las importancias del comercia, porque es claro, y consecuente que cuanto más se franquea el tráfico a los extranjeros, tanto más se disminuye, e imposibilita, el que hacen o habían de hacer los propios vasallos, en sus navíos y porque de algunos a esta parte se hallan excluidos de este gran beneficio, se ha seguido la despoblación, pobreza, y otras calamidades que se padecen en España a vista de las riquezas, abundancias, y fuerzas superiores que con nuestros desperdicios logran las demás naciones. (*Papeles Varios* 170v–171)

The first of which is that it is against the laws, and royal decrees do not need any more justification than that of reading of the books and notebooks in which royal orders are compiled and printed out ... Second because royal interests are damaged, and the vassals, which also wouldn't need much explanation if the rules were more commonly known in Spain, and [third] because of the importance of commerce, because it is clear and consequential that the more trade is given to the foreigners, the more what is done or was done by the vassals themselves, in their vessels, is reduced and prevented, and because some of them find themselves excluded from this benefit, Spain has been plagued by depopulation, poverty, and other calamities, particularly in comparison to the riches, abundance, and superior forces which other nations achieve because of our waste. (Trans. RG & EC)

By the time these documents are written in 1720, the chocolate trade is so important to Spain that they believe not only that it would be legally difficult to circumvent previous laws and decrees but also that it would be detrimental economically to Spain, from the highest echelons to the poorest of its citizens. The paper concludes by pointing out that if supply were as low as is being proposed, there would be far less available to the citizens of Madrid, where demand is high, but, as "kilometro cero" of Spain, importation from the coasts is also more difficult and therefore expensive. This is not, however, the case at all, since "en Madrid se halla cacao bueno a ocho reales la libra y más barato comprándolo por arrobas cuyo precio es el mismo que tenía en tiempo de Paz, y hay personas que aseguran que en esta Corte y en sus contornos se hallan almacenados cerca de dos millones de libras, sin las cantidades que hay en las tiendas" ("in Madrid one finds good cacao at eight *reales* per pound and even cheaper buying it in 'arrojas,' whose price is the same as in the time of Peace, and there are people who claim that the court and its outliers are themselves stocked up with near two million pounds, without counting the quantities found in stores"; 172v; trans. RG & EC). If in Madrid there is no desperate need, there is unlikely to be need anywhere else in Spain, either.

By the mid-1700s, the fervour of chocolate consumption had levelled out. Although it remained popular and was considered the hospitable choice to offer to guests, there was plenty to go around. Enough that, when it was once again suggested that cacao be allowed to enter freely into Spain, without importation fees, in approximately 1718,[28] the King's councillors responded that they were already picking more than could be consumed in the provinces and the market would be flooded by foreign products while Spanish merchants would be undersold and undercut in every way (*Papeles Varios* 409–11). As Irene Fattacciu demonstrates, the importation of chocolate was on the rise in the eighteenth century (66), and prices dropped consistently enough to enable the middle classes to partake in it, at least occasionally (74). She cites the case of a government employee who, out of his yearly salary of twenty-five thousand *reales*, devoted at least one thousand *reales* to the consumption of chocolate and other sweets for himself and his family of ten (74). By the time de la Cruz's ten-volume compendium of plays and interludes was published between 1786 and 1791, it was so commonplace that he included it in twelve of the sixty-five pieces, sometimes in passing, sometimes as a major plot point.[29]

Within a century, chocolate had transformed from a symbol of alterity to one of status, and finally to an everyday commodity that even the lowliest of people could indulge in. Such a rapid transformation left in its wake a slew of documents, legal, historical, and literary, that speak to the various ways in which the drink could be seen, employed, and commodified for everyone, from the *indiano* seeking his place in Spanish society, to the high-society women trying to build an intellectual and social community for themselves, to members of the lower classes, who wished to drink from the same cup and emulate those they served. One final, anonymous literary source, *Coplas nuevas para que sepan del modo que se toma el chocolate*, likely written in the early part of the nineteenth century, demonstrates just how widespread and commonplace the consumption of chocolate had become. The couplets enumerate all of the people who now drink chocolate regularly, from "niñas del barrio" ("street girls") to "medicos y cirujanos" ("doctors and surgeons") to "soldados" ("soldiers") and "sastres y zapateros" ("tailors and shoemakers"; 1–2). Although the poem never elaborates on how to actually drink chocolate, it does make it clear that people of all walks of life are, by that time, imbibing.

CHAPTER 4

Chocolate in the Church: Ecclesiastical Debates on Chocolate and Fasting

This chapter will consider how chocolate was viewed by the Church as it became a more important commodity in Spain throughout the seventeenth century. As we will see, there was considerable concern over the incorporation of chocolate into a culture centred on the Catholic faith. Particularly, a debate arose regarding the use of chocolate during days of fast, a practice that was fairly common in the Catholic Church of the early modern period. Responses varied, and the differing perspectives are key to understanding how contemporary Spaniards viewed Indigenous culture as both fascinating and dangerous at the same time. Throughout the seventeenth century, chocolate moves from the realm of the symbolic outsider into the centre, as a common practice that links Spain to its colonies and vice versa. Although a number of literary sources will be incorporated, there is one play – *Santa Rosa del Perú* (1671) by Agustín Moreto and Pedro Lanini y Sagredo, which celebrates the beatification of the first saint of the Americas – that will be analysed extensively for its demonstration of the incorporation of chocolate into religious practices, while at the same time it both exoticizes and suppresses the drink's Otherness.

In order to understand just how important this debate could have been within seventeenth-century Spanish society, we need to explore the rules and regulations surrounding fasting in the Catholic Church. The practice was a continuation of that of the Middle Ages, and there were approximately 150 fast days a year, including Lent. Ken Albala explains that this practice was generally not a total fast, but that, for example, "all healthy individuals were expected to abstain from all animal flesh and products obtained from animals such as milk, butter or eggs, for the entire period of Lent. They were also technically supposed to eat only one meal a day during Lent" (196). Interestingly, fasting became even more central to Catholic doctrine during and after the Reformation and Counter-Reformation, in spite of complaints of papal corruption in the selling of fasting dispensations (Albala 200–1).

Antonio de Leon Pinelo, the theologian who falls most strongly into the faction against chocolate as an acceptable fasting beverage, compartmentalizes fasts into four different categories in his 1636 *Questión moral: Si el chocolate quebranta el ayuno eclesiástico*:

> La primera el ayuno espiritual, que es la abstinencia de vicios y pecados ... La segunda el moral, o la abstinencia, que prohíbe comidas y bebidas escusadas y demasiadas, y es opuesta a la gula, y embriaguez, como advierten los sumistas. La tercera la abstinencia o ayuno natural, que se requiere en los sanos para la sagrada comunión. La cuarta, la abstinencia, o ayuno eclesiástico, que se guarda en los días que por precepto de la iglesia, o votos particulares están declarados por deste ayuno. (Fol. 9v–10r)

> The first is the spiritual fast, which is abstaining from vices and sins ... The second is the moral, which prohibits foods and drinks that are excused, and all the rest, which is the opposite of gluttony, and intoxication, just as the moralists advise. The third is the natural fast, which is required in healthy people for sacred communion. The fourth, or ecclesiastical fast, is held on the days that by mandate of the church, or particular votes, have been declared for fasting.

For Pinelo, the fourth or ecclesiastical category is the most important one to consider when thinking about the uses of chocolate. During such fasts, drinks are permitted, but *essential* food is not. Whether or not a food or drink is essential depends upon its intrinsic form. Pinelo gives the following example:

> ... como lo vemos en un bizcocho, que aunque se deshaga en agua, o en vino, y se beba en diferente forma y calidad, quebrantará el ayuno. Y el agua aunque se hiele, o hecha nieve, o granizo se coma, no le quebrantará, por ser estas mutaciones, y conversiones extrínsecas y accidentales, no intrínsecas, ni esenciales, como lo serán si el vino cociéndole se convierte en arrope, o las uvas exprimiéndolas se convierten en vino. (Fol. 11v)

> ... as we can see in a cake, that, even if it were dissolved in water, or in wine, and it were drunk in a different form and quality, it would still break the fast. And water, even if it froze, or became snow, or ice, and were eaten, it would not break it, because these mutations and conversions are extrinsic and accidental, not intrinsic or essential, just as it would be if cooking wine turned it into a reduction, or if pressing grapes turned them to wine.

The essential function of the extrinsic conversion, for Pinelo, is one that does not convert the nutritive quality of the food in question. Thus, those changes, such as breaking up a cake and dissolving in water, do not remove the nutrients – or what we might now call calories – of the food itself. If the food, even in drink form, is still nutritious or caloric enough to give us the strength to carry on with our day, it would violate the Church's mandates on fasting, a process that Pinelo reminds us the Church requires "o para reparar la culpa, o para disponer la gracia, solo pretende mortificar y enflaquecer los cuerpos, para que menos llevadas de sus afectos, queden más libres las almas, y así no nos prohíbe la bebida, que no sustenta el cuerpo, y tiempla el exceso de su calor natural, para que no nos consuma y acabe; sino la comida como causa inmediata de las fuerzas y vigor" ("either in order to fix sin or give grace, only intending to mortify and weaken the bodies, so that, less encumbered by their effects, the souls are left freer, and thus the Church does not prohibit us from drink, that does not sustain the body, and moderates the excesses of its natural heat, so that we are not consumed and killed by it; but only from food, as the immediate cause of strength and vigour"; fol. 25r).

On the other side of the ecclesiastical debate, Tomás Hurtado likely would not argue with the Church's reasoning for having fast days, but he does take almost all of Pinelo's arguments against chocolate during the fast and turns them around to prove the worthiness of chocolate as a fasting supplement. As previously mentioned, Pinelo argues that chocolate is by nature a food, even when turned into a drink. He continues this line of thinking, stating that chocolate "no es bebida simple, ni natural como el agua, ni compuesta como el vino, aloja, cerveza, cidra, ni otras que se hacen por distilación, expresión, o infusión de cosas comestibles, y materiales, y se convierten en esencialmente potables" ("it is not a simple drink, not natural such as water, nor a composite, such as wine, aloja, beer, cider, or any others that are made by the distillation, expression, or infusion of edible materials, and are then converted into essential potables"; fol. 22r–22v). Although Hurtado agrees that the actual solid version cannot be eaten during times of fast, he argues in *Chocolate y tabaco, ayuno eclesiástico y natural* (1645) that chocolate is essentially a drink and not a food by relying in part on idiomatic expressions: "pues así en las Indias, como en España, no se dice comer una jícara de Chocolate, sino beber una jícara de Chocolate" ("thus in the Indies, as in Spain, it is not said that you eat a *jícara* of Chocolate, but rather drink a *jícara* of Chocolate"; fol. 4).[1] He goes so far as to reverse Pinelo's example of pressed grapes:

Últimamente convienen todos, que si la pasta de Chocolate, que se deshace en agua, se come, quebranta el ayuno, porque pierde la forma de bebida, como si uno come un racimo de uvas, que pese una libra, sin duda quebranta el ayuno; pero no si le exprime, y se bebe el mosto; y lo mismo si come las manzanas de que se hace la cerveza, y no le quebranta si se bebe una, ni muchas azumbres della. (Fol. 3)

Ultimately everyone agrees that if the chocolate paste, which is dissolved in water, is eaten, it would break the fast, because it loses its drinkable form, just as if one ate a bunch of grapes that weigh a pound it would break the fast without doubt; but not if they are pressed, and the juice were drunk; and the same if one eats the apples from which beer is made, but [the fast] would not be broken if one drank one or many of them [beers].

In fact, Hurtado admits that chocolate, like wine, does give some sustenance to the body; however, chocolate for him is just a drink unless mixed with other comestibles such as milk or eggs – not entirely out of the question for the practices of the day – because those are actually life sustaining and nutritive. But he argues that chocolate itself, mixed with water, and perhaps some sugar and spices, is not in and of itself capable of breaking the fast. And even if it is, the breaking is accidental and not intentional, and thus does not count (fol. 3–5). Intention is key for Hurtado:

Y si uno la toma para que le sustente, quien duda que quebranta el ayuno ... el acto exterior imperado desta intención es opuesto al ley del ayuno, y lo mismo se ha de decir del beber vino, si se bebe, en cuanto sustenta y nutre, y es mucha la cantidad que se bebe: porque la costumbre que hay de beber vino, es en cuanto satisface la sed, y ayuda a la digestión de los manjares ... (Fol. 11–12)

And if one were to drink it so that it sustained him, who would doubt that it breaks the fast ... the dominating exterior act of this intention is the opposite of the fasting laws, and the same would have to be said about drinking wine, if it is drunk in so far as it sustains and nourishes, which would have to be a large quantity drunk: because the custom that exists in drinking wine is in so far as it satisfies thirst, and helps with the digestion of food ...

For Hurtado perhaps the strongest argument for the use of chocolate during days of fast is that of habit. Going back to Saint Thomas, a new custom would be tolerated within Church doctrine when it was used by many people, and when forty years had passed without complaint. Once both of those two conditions are met, the new custom becomes very difficult to repeal, even if it has been founded in error (fol. 17–18). Hurtado concludes that chocolate is a natural drink, and one that has been in customary use for over forty years, and thus falls into the category of always-already allowed (fol. 19). Interestingly, Pinelo also refers to the requisite forty years, but denies that consuming chocolate has existed as a custom long enough to comply with the doctrine: "Que esta costumbre de que tratamos sea contra Derecho, queda probado; luego requiere cuarenta años para prescribirse: los cuales no solo en España no han pasado, donde no ha diez que el Chocolate se bebe en común, pero ni en las Indias; aunque es en ellas tan antiguo" ("That the custom about which we are speaking is against the Law has been proved; then it requires forty years in order to be enacted: the likes of which have not only not passed in Spain, where it has not been even ten years that chocolate has been commonly drunk, but also not in the Indies, even though there it is much older"; fol. 78r). In fact, Pinelo reminds the reader that even if it were the custom in the Indies, that does not make the act virtuous for Spaniards:

Los Indios con su uso no nos pueden dar consecuencia: porque ni ellos guardaban abstinencia de manjares en días ciertos, ni se les prohibían ningunos, ni tenían el precepto del ayuno eclesiástico. Luego no podemos hacer argumento de sus comidas, ni bebidas, para nuestro uso y religión. Las más naciones de las Indias comían carne humana, y siendo de las muy políticas la Mexicana, aun a sus Reyes se servía en los convites por plato extraordinario y de regalo ... (Fol. 16r–16v)

The Indians, with their use, cannot be taken seriously by us: since they neither maintained abstinence of food in certain days, nor were they prohibited anything, nor did they have the concept of ecclesiastical fasting. Thus can we not make justifications of their foods, or drinks, for our use and religion. The majority of Indian nations ate human flesh, and in Mexico it was served in banquets as an extraordinary plate, gifted even to the Kings ...

Pinelo purposely brings up the most reviled Indigenous practice, cannibalism, in order to remind his Spanish audience of how barbaric, and therefore untrustworthy, the Indigenous peoples are. This may not have been a calculated move on his part, but we must be careful not to take the colonial perspective on the tenuous links between cannibalism and Indigenous communities. By doing so, Pinelo does not have to make any logical arguments; chocolate is now related to the Indigenous people and their practices, like cannibalism, that can never be accepted by God-fearing Christians. As Earle demonstrates, this was a common belief about the Americas and their inhabitants, in some cases used to justify violence against Indigenous communities, and yet it was quite possibly overblown ("Spaniards, Cannibals, and the Eucharist" 82–4).[2] Pinelo continues this line of thinking, arguing that Spaniards, being ruled by Christian law and "natural reason," could not possibly admit such a food – that is, human flesh – and therefore they also cannot allow themselves to follow any other practices that might imitate those of the Indigenous, barbaric people. If they do allow themselves to be lulled into practices that originated in the New World, they cannot do so "sin quedar por más bárbaros que ellos" ("without becoming more barbarous than them"; fol. 16v). His argument is that if they do it, we cannot. It is odd, then, that he goes on to tell us that in fact the Indigenous inventors themselves do not use or permit chocolate in their own "ayunos bárbaros sin forma, ley, ni merito" ("barbaric fasts without structure, law, or merit"; fol. 18r), and thus Christians should be even more wary of them. Apparently

Pinelo's condemnation of Indigenous practices only extends so far as they contradict his own convictions.[3]

Hurtado does not directly refer to the Indigenous practices to prove his point; however, he does equate chocolate to other drinks already allowed within Church fasting practices, namely wine and *electuarios* – medicinal drinks made up of various herbs mixed with honey and water – which were seen not as sustaining, but rather as either medicinal digestive aids or thirst quenchers (fol. 5). For Hurtado, successful fasting is much more dependent on people's intentions than on their specific actions. *Electuarios* were allowed, as was wine, because they were seen to have a medicinal effect. Hurtado links chocolate to these already allowed drinks, citing theologians such as Saint Thomas to demonstrate their harmless nature during the fast:

> Todo he dicho, para que el que toma electuarios, bebe Chocolate, o vino, siguiendo la opinión de los antiguos, que tengo explicada, advierta la intención que debe tener para no pecar, que ha de ser mirando a estas cosas, no como son nutritivas, y satisfacen el hambre, sino como satisfacen la sed, ayudan a la digestión, y alteran el cuerpo. (Fol. 12–13)

> Everything I have said so long as he who drinks *electuarios*, chocolate, or wine, according to the opinion of the ancient [writers], as I have explained, observes the intention not to sin; so we have to look at these things, not as they are nutritious, or satisfy hunger, [but] rather as they satisfy thirst, help digestion, and alter the body.

Thus, if one only intends to drink chocolate for a medicinal or digestive effect, Hurtado allows it – even if it actually is sustaining to the body – because the intention is more important than the actual outcome.

The average early modern Spanish citizen would likely not have access to – or in many cases the ability to read – Pinelo's or Hurtado's treatises on the appropriateness of chocolate during the fast. Yet, the average person attempting to follow the Church mandates to the best of their abilities may have been looking for an answer to this very question. Thus, to consider how the layperson might have understood fasting, we will look to literature, particularly the *comedia*, as a potential source of information for those who did not have access to official documents. The first conquest plays focus on the alterity and danger that the New World symbolized and, as such, emphasize the actions of the Indigenous people that would be considered strange and titillating for the audience in Spain. It is not until late in the seventeenth century that we find plays set in the Americas that centre on the lives of the Creole inhabitants. In the 1660s, the Catholic Church was set to beatify the first American saint and had decided on Isabel Flores de Oliva, who would become known as Santa Rosa del Perú or Santa Rosa de Lima. Her beatification represented a shift in the prevailing opinion of the New World, and Agustin Moreto was commissioned to write a play commemorating her life and her role in saving Lima from invading Indigenous armies. Although he was unable to finish the play before his death, it was completed by one of his protégés, Pedro Lanini y Sagredo.

Food is one of the main symbols of this play, with a particular focus on the uses of chocolate. The plot is driven by the machinations of Rosa's father to marry her off to a rich *perulero* – that is, a Spaniard who has made substantial amounts of money while conquering Peru – and her potential husband's desire to prove himself worthy of her against an unknown adversary. Little does he know that the "unknown adversary" is the devil in disguise, who believes that if he can trick the devout Rosa into taking a husband or lover he will eradicate the hold Catholicism has on the Creole inhabitants and retain his rule over the Americas.

Food also plays an important role as it intertwines the Catholic and Indigenous traditions, playing the part of both religious offering and exotic symbol, often at the same time. Rosa – like most good protagonists of any early modern Spanish play – has a *gracioso* or servant who provides comic relief. In this case our *gracioso*'s name is Bodigo.

Everything about Bodigo is created to remind the audience of food, including his name, which is also the name given to small loaves of bread made as church offerings. In practically every speech he makes, he talks about food, complains about fasting, or uses food-related metaphors about the people around him.

Chocolate plays a central role in Rosa's fictitious salvation. In the theatrical version, *Santa Rosa del Perú*, Rosa takes small amounts of chocolate, which she considers medicinal. She also uses it to alleviate her passions and keep her on the path to righteousness. Chocolate is the first fully transatlantic food, that is, one that was eaten – and even modified – on both sides of the Atlantic soon after the encounter between the New and Old Worlds, and it carries cultural and social connotations from both Spanish and Indigenous traditions. For the pre-conquest Indigenous peoples, chocolate was highly valued and served not only as a drink but also as money, and in some cases, as a stand-in for blood in sacrificial ceremonies. It was also possibly used as an aphrodisiac, as we have seen in previous chapters, and as will be discussed further herein. For the Spaniards, it was exotic, with both religious and sexual connotations, and yet, at the time of the play's writing, it was also becoming commonplace in Spanish households, especially among the nobility. The use of chocolate within the play, therefore, serves both as the symbolic – or what Christopher Gascón calls "synecdochal" (46) – exoticism that entices the audience and as a site of theatrical identification between the audience and the first Creole saint. Rosa, as a Creole character whose concerns seem to be far more linked to the peninsula than they are to her own continent, stands in for the Spaniard as a good Catholic woman trying to remain as close as possible to God, while her servant, Bodigo, for whom the biggest concerns are those most basic to survival, is symbolic of the Other. Rosa, then, might be satiated by her medicinal helping of chocolate, but Bodigo's appetite is far greater, and he misinterprets every word spoken by his mistress as a reminder of another mouth-watering dish. Bodigo's misinterpretations serve as a memorial of the foods that were popular in early modern Spain and its American colonies while also reminding the audience of the play's exotic setting.

The third act of the play, which is the act most critics consider to have been written by Lanini y Sagredo after Moreto's death, centres on Rosa's and Bodigo's fasting. Rosa fasts as a sort of mortification of the flesh from within, believing that any pain it causes her will bring her closer to God. Bodigo fasts because Rosa does – she refuses any food, and since he is always with her, he does not receive meals either. Having fasted to the point that they are both almost delirious with pain, Rosa tells Bodigo of a dream in which the Virgin Mary came to her. Bodigo also had a dream, but his is "en una fuente / de pepitoria de pavo" ("in a fountain of turkey stew"; jornada 3). Although the idea of turkey stew might seem strange when we consider that stew – especially "pepitoria" as he calls it here – was a traditional Spanish preparation of meat and vegetables, while turkey was an American bird, yet we know that turkey was one of the foods that quickly made the jump across the pond, as evidenced by its inclusion in an English cookbook from 1594–7, *The good Huswifes Handmaide for the Kitchin*.[4] He also uses the Castilian word for turkey: *pavo*. In Mexico, to this day, you can hear it called *guajolote*, derived from the Nahuatl *huexolotl*. In the volume *Conquista y comida: Consecuencias del encuentro de dos mundos*, Xavier Domingo tells us that medieval sauces were quickly adapted to New World birds (27), while Doris Heyden and Ana María L. Velasco note that "En Europa estas aves no interesaron como rareza culinaria ya que había otras similares ... en cambio el *huexolotl* fue bien recibido y adornó, como aquí, las mesas de la elite" ("In Europe these birds were not seen as a culinary rarity since there were already similar ones there ... in fact, the *huexolotl* was well received and adorned, just as it did here [Mexico], the tables of the elite"; 252). We see that it was indeed well received by the early part of the seventeenth century, when Gonzalo Correas wrote his book of popular refrains, in which he annotates a saying in which the interlocutor refuses to share: "Lo primero dice el que ve alguna buena cosa de comer como pavo" ("That first part is said by him who sees something wonderful to eat, like turkey"; 317).[5] Much like chocolate, turkey quickly becomes a transatlantic commodity, enjoyed on both sides of the ocean.

Shortly after this exchange, the "niño Jesus" ("baby Jesus") appears to Rosa, and they play a game of dice, which Jesus wins. What he wins is more pain for Rosa, which she happily accepts, in spite of its being so intense that she cries out and wakes the entire house. She finally consents to drink a small amount of chocolate. Bodigo, ever vigilant for the possibility of a meal, jumps at the opportunity to promote the benefits of chocolate: "Es cosa rica, / y su más hidalgo apodo / es que es un sánalo todo / y no le hay en la botica" ("It is a delicious thing, and its best quality is that it is a cure-all, the likes of which you won't find in the pharmacy"; jornada 3). Bodigo and Rosa's father, Gaspar, discuss what is to be done: it is the middle of the night and there is no chocolate in the house. Bodigo promises Gaspar that he knows how to make it from scratch, while Rosa claims that someone (Jesus) has already sent for it. Gaspar and Bodigo cannot understand how "someone" could have gone for it if no one has left the house and continue trying to make their own out of nothing. Bodigo calls himself "santo jicarero," referring to the jars, or "jícaras," used in the seventeenth century to serve chocolate, and proceeds to explain how to make it:

Ya está el agua a calentar,
ya el recado van a echar,
ya baten el molinillo,
ya lo traen hacia acá,
para que a Rosa consuele.
Ya llega a casa, y ya huele,
mira que tan cerca está.
Ya entra, para que le den
las gracias de lo que pasa. (Jornada 3)

Now the water is on to boil, now the spices will be thrown in, now the chocolate mill churns,[6] now they bring it here, so that it might console Rosa. Now it arrives, and now it can be smelled, look how close it is. Now it enters, so that it might be given the thanks for what is happening.

A servant arrives at the house, carrying a *chocolatera* – the vessel used to make chocolate (see image 4.1)[7] – sent as if by magic, or, perhaps, divine intervention by a neighbour to help Rosa through her pain. When the servant invokes the name of God to bless the inhabitants of the house, Bodigo is quick to remind them that chocolate is just as necessary: "Criado. Sea Dios en esta casa. / Bodigo. Y el chocolate también" ("Servant. May God be in this house. Bodigo. And chocolate as well"; jornada 3). In spite of these potentially heretical remarks, they both drink the chocolate. Rosa confesses its healing properties to Bodigo: "Solo puede esta bebida / quebrantarme este dolor" ("It is the only drink that can dull my pain"; jornada 3). He replies with fascination: "¿Hay cosa como un licor tal, / que quebranta un dolor, / y no quebranta el ayuno?" ("Is there anything better than such a drink that can break pain and yet not break the fast?"; jornada 3). In this short phrase Bodigo refers directly to the ideas espoused by Pinelo and Hurtado – falling obviously on the Hurtado side of the debate – regarding the nutritional and spiritual value of chocolate.[8] Calderón de la Barca makes the same claim, with a slight twist, in *El pésame de la viuda* (1651): "bebida tan regalada / que no quebranta el ayuno, / a la viudedad quebranta" ("such a sumptuous drink, that does not break the fast, but does break widowhood"; lines 58–60).

Aside from the fast-breaking debate, there were also questions regarding the moral value of chocolate for one so chaste as Santa Rosa. The historical episode in Santa Rosa's life from which this scene was adapted was also cited in the ongoing debate by an Italian theologian, Gudenfridi:

... we are told that one day, after many hours of an ardent elevation of spirits, the Holy Girl, feeling herself languish, lacking breath, and weakened in body, had at her side an Angel, who presented her with a little cup

Figure 4.1 *Still Life with an Ebony Chest* (1652) by Antonio de Pereda. This still life from the mid-seventeenth century appears to represent the table of an *indiano* recently returned from the New World – although, according to Rafael Romero Asenjo, the ebony chest is likely one that belonged to the painter himself (297) – complete with a *chocolatera* and *molinillo* on the left-hand side, behind porcelain serving cups and an ornately decorated *jícara* on top of the chest, to the right, as well as some small pieces of bread, similar to the *bodigo* after which the *gracioso* in *Santa Rosa del Perú* is named (courtesy of The State Hermitage Museum, St Petersburg).

of chocolate, with which she regained her vigor and her strength returned. I ask the Sig. Cav. Felini what he thinks of this angel? Does he think it is an angel of darkness, or of light? Bad or good? He cannot think it bad without offense, to say the least, of the trust due to the historian. But, if it was a good one, does he think that if Chocolate be the poison of chastity, that the Angel would have brought it to a Virgin of Christ? If Chocolate injects into the veins of those that drink it the spirit of lasciviousness, does he think that the good Angel would have given even a sip to a maiden who was a Temple of the Holy Spirit? (Qtd by Coe and Coe 154)

In spite of Gudenfridi's chaste interpretation of chocolate, there were plenty of anecdotes that would imply the opposite. The idea that chocolate served an erotic purpose was promoted by the very first encounters with the drink by Hernán Cortés and his soldiers: Upon arriving in the Aztec city of Tenochtitlan, one of Cortés's soldiers, Díaz del Castillo, observed the Aztec leader Montezuma drinking chocolate and understood two things: one, that chocolate was reserved for the elite members of Mesoamerican society, and two, that it was a purported aphrodisiac. Even though issues of translation and perception might be at play in Díaz del Castillo's observation, the idea that chocolate was linked to exoticism and eroticism was one that persisted in the Spanish consciousness, and it will be touched on further in chapter 6. Here, however, we find that the play promotes the medicinal properties, as the chocolate not only cures Rosa's stomach pains but also some of Bodigo's ailments, and he believes it could go so far as to be an antidote to old age, offering it to Rosa's father:

¡Jesús! También me ha sanado
a mí una muela podrida.
Su crédito desta vez
adelanta mucho el paso.
Tómale tú, por si acaso
te sana de la vejez. (Jornada 3)

Jesus! It has also cured my rotten tooth. It has gone above and beyond
its reputation. Take some, in case it can cure you of old age.

When Gaspar refuses his share, Bodigo is happy to double up on the
cure for his own ailments.

The pain itself denotes the difference between the religious Rosa
and the irreverent Bodigo. While his pain stems entirely from his corporeal being – the rotten tooth, his constant hunger – Rosa is convinced that her pain comes from God, as a test or punishment. This
was, in fact, the point of fasting, according to Pinelo: "porque como
el hambre, y la sed, sean cierto género de dolor, y el padecer dolor sea
especie de penitencia, fue muy justo padeciese el hombre este tal dolor
en descuento de sus culpas y pecados; de suerte que según esto, aquel
se dirá más verdaderamente ayunar, que mayor dolor de sed y hambre
padeciere por Dios" ("because, as hunger and thirst are a certain genre
of pain, and feeling pain is a type of penitence, it was just that man
might feel such a pain in compensation for his faults and sins; as such,
that which has the most pain of thirst and hunger will be said to be the
truer fast for God"; 114r). Throughout the play Rosa complains of a
pain deep in her stomach, but often refuses to receive help or take any
kind of medication, as it is "un dolor sabroso" ("a delicious pain";
jornada 3) that was given to her by Jesus, whom she calls her "dulce
esposo" ("sweet husband") on numerous occasions. Rosa's pain can
be interpreted as desire as well, as indicated in an earlier scene, in
which Rosa is visited by the devil and Don Juan, who are almost successful in their plan to seduce her. As Juan enters her room and begins
his attempted seduction, she cries out "¿Qué fuego es este que estaba
/ dentro del alma escondido, / dulce Esposo?" ("What fire is this that
was hidden deep in my soul, sweet Husband?"; jornada 2). Although
"sweet Husband" refers to Jesus, the fire she refers to is one awoken
by the caresses of Juan. Rosa has felt human touch – and lust – for the
first time. At the last moment she calls out for "el niño Jesus," and he
comes to her rescue, along with an angel. Because he only visits her in

infant form, Rosa can withdraw from any lingering feelings of sexuality back to her understanding of the world through religious terms. Rosa, desexualized as she is through her religious vocation, can only relate to "el niño Jesus," not to the man her father wishes her to marry or even to Jesus in adult form, in spite of her continuous references to him as her husband. Given this scene, and the "pain" that it awakens in her, one might infer that the use of chocolate later to dull the pain given to her by Jesus is being used not, in fact, to cure pain but to cure desire. Chocolate was believed to cure women's ailments – and was also thought to be able to rid one of desire (Gamboa 36), something that would have been concerning for a would-be saint.

The scene in which Rosa uses chocolate to quell her stomach can be interpreted as a hybridization of the Indigenous and Spanish understandings of religious rituals and the use of chocolate within them, as Gascón has so articulately demonstrated:

> Mayans anointed boys and girls with chocolate during a ritual resembling the Christian baptism. Though Rosa is not literally baptized in the scene in question, she could be compared to the subject of a rite of passage: God tests her fortitude by making her endure pain but helps her in her change of status from the human to the divine by giving her chocolate. Mayans also used grains of cacao as a symbol of betrothal in marriage ceremonies. The idea of marriage is present in this scene: Jesus has appeared to Rosa, who addresses him as her "dulce Esposo" [sweet husband] ... (Gascón 50–1)

The connection is further made by Bodigo, who, upon hearing that Rosa will finally take chocolate to alleviate her pain, calls it an "ofrenda" ("offering"), which, as Mirzam Pérez points out, can be interpreted as a reference to the Aztec usage, and as a reminder of the status of chocolate as "a God-given prize for Spain and a fair retribution for the conquest of the American lands" (Pérez 101). Although Gascón and Pérez point to different cultural traditions – neither of which, it must be noted, is related to Peru, where Rosa's life and story take place – the Spanish authors of these texts would not have been very aware of the vast differences between the pre-Columbian peoples and cultures, and likely assumed there to be a Pan-American experience that they could apply to their literary interpretations of events. We know now that the use of cacao in the Andes would have been very different from that of Mesoamerica, and from the depiction in this play, but that was of little concern to Agustín and Lanini y Sagredo.[9]

Furthering the interpretation of chocolate as religious offering, at the end of the scene Bodigo is content to finish up any leftovers that the others have neglected, and when asked by Rosa what he is doing he replies "Empapar / el bodigo en chocolate" ("Soaking the *bodigo* in chocolate"; jornada 3). Bodigo in this case could be referring to his name, but also to the bread used as an offering in the Catholic Church. Although the use of chocolate as a part of Church offerings might seem sacrilegious to us, it was not uncommon in the early colonial period. As we have seen, cacao beans were so highly regarded, especially by the Indigenous community, that they were used as currency. In order to subsume Indigenous customs into Catholicism, a "Señor del cacao" or "Christ of the Cacao Bean" (see image 4.2) was erected in the Cathedral of Mexico City so that Indigenous converts could continue the practice of leaving cacao beans as an offering to God (Aguilar-Moreno 275–6). Chocolate was also seen as a substitute for blood sacrifice in some pre-Columbian cultures: coloured with a spice called "achiote," it turned red and looked like blood, was considered a cure for haemorrhages, and became a part of marriage ceremonies (Norton 1).

Chocolate serves to remind the audience that the play is set in the New World, a symbol that stands in for the alterity they would have come to expect in such a setting, and yet its exoticism is tempered through its medicinal use by the woman who would soon become the first American saint: Santa Rosa herself, in becoming the first American saint, is being used to downplay the exoticism of the New World.

Figure 4.2 "El señor del cacao" ("Christ of the Cacao Bean"), sixteenth century, in the San José Chapel of the Metropolitan Cathedral of Mexico City (courtesy of Anagoria, under the GNU Free Documentation License).

Although there were several non-Creole Catholics who were being considered at the time for that honour, ultimately it is Rosa, a Creole woman with Spanish parents, who is beatified first (Gascón 52–3). Thus Rosa and her life story are used, both on stage and historically, to normalize the New World.[10]

Bodigo, on the other hand, serves as an almost ridiculous counterpoint to Rosa's piety. For as much as she sings the praises of God, he revels in his basest instincts, turning everyone else's words into reminders of food and feasting. When Rosa believes that she has missed a chance to speak with Jesus while sleeping, she laments, "¡Oh, qué dulzura tan bella / perdí por estar dormida!" ("Oh what lovely sweetness have I missed, having been asleep!"; jornada 3). Bodigo, of course, assumes that she is talking about a sweet food, not a sweet moment or person, and so he is also upset, promising to look for it and asking for a description: "¿Vino en seco o en almíbar?" ("Did it come dry or in syrup?"; jornada 3). What follows is a comedic scene that comments on the misunderstandings that come between two people who are both single-minded, but regarding entirely different goals, with Rosa's focus on the eternal and Bodigo's on the temporal:

ROSA. Vino en la misma hermosura,
   y con dulce melodía
   llamó hasta que despertamos.
BODIGO. Pues sigámosla, aunque vamos
   hasta la confitería.
ROSA. El olor sólo provoca
   a estimar sus maravillas.
BODIGO. Por aquí huele a pastillas,
   pero no a cosa de boca.
ROSA. Dulces del alma lisonjas,
   ¿dónde os fuisteis?
BODIGO. Lindo cuento;
   se habrán ido a algún convento,
   que el dulce anda entre las monjas.

ROSA. Llamémosle pues, Bodigo.

Tenga esperanza esta pena.

BODIGO. Llamémosle en hora buena.

ROSA. Divino Amor ...

BODIGO. Buen amigo ...

ROSA. Dulce y fiel amigo mío ...

BODIGO. ¿Dulce en caja o en bocado?

...

Venga dulce, aunque sea frío. (Jornada 3)

ROSA. It came with the same beauty, and with a sweet melody, called out until it woke us.

BODIGO. Well, let's follow it, even if it takes us all the way to the confectionary.

ROSA. The smell only provokes the estimation of its miracles.

BODIGO. Around here it smells like soap, but not of anything you would eat.

ROSA. Delighting sweets of the soul, where did you go?

BODIGO. What a story; they will have gone to some convent, the sweet walks among the nuns.

ROSA. Let us call them, Bodigo. This pain has hope.

BODIGO. Let's call them, before it is too late.

ROSA. Divine love ...

BODIGO. Good friend ...

ROSA. Sweet and loyal friend of mine ...

BODIGO. Sweets, by the box or mouthful? ... Come back, even if cold.

The confusion, as they search for the missing "sweetness," comes from their inability to communicate on each other's level and is indicative of the bigger picture – which is to say, the Spanish Empire. Rosa, concerned only with her devotion to her "husband," Jesus, to whom she wishes to devote her life, represents Spain's mission to convert the people of the New World for the growth and prosperity of the Catholic Church. Bodigo, on the other hand, is only able to focus on his bodily functions and has no apparent concept of the divine, representing the conception of the New World inhabitants as heathens, non-Christians who could not possibly have a deeper spiritual life of their own. Although there is no direct indication of Bodigo's origins within the play, his status as a servant in a Spanish American colonial household would suggest a potential link to Indigenous, African, or *mestizo* ancestry. In any case, and unfortunately for Bodigo, their efforts do not succeed in finding anything to eat, but Jesus does reappear to Rosa.

Although much of the talk of chocolate and sweets appears in Lanini y Sagredo's third act, the original author, Moreto, sets the scene for Bodigo's outrageous food-based misunderstandings from the beginning, including, as discussed, his very name. In the second act, when Gonzalo, Juan's confidant, discusses Rosa's habit of mortification with Bodigo, Bodigo explains that mortification is like sustenance to her:

> BODIGO. Eso no le quitarán
> los azotes que se casca,
> aunque la echen a galeras.
> GONZALO. ¿Pues por qué?
> BODIGO. Porque mandarla
> que no se azote, es mandar
> a un cochero beber agua:
> los azotes son sus dulces. (Jornada 2)

> BODIGO. Nothing will stop the lashes she gives herself, even if they threw
> her in the galleys.
> GONZALO. But why?
> BODIGO. Because asking her not to flog herself is like asking a coachman
> to drink water: lashes are her sweets.

The insinuation is that Rosa is addicted to self-flagellation as a coach driver is to alcohol. Finally, they discuss that which most affects

Bodigo: fasting. Since servants often ate their masters' leftovers, Bodigo complains that there cannot be anything left over when there was nothing eaten in the first place:

> ROSA. Yo lo que he menester como,
>   lo demás no me hace falta.
> BODIGO. Pero me hace falta a mí,
>   que los crïados se hartan
>   de lo que sobra a los amos,
>   y el pobre Bodigo anda
>   siempre royéndose el nombre,
>   porque jamás sobra nada.
> ROSA. Tú come lo que quisieres.
> BODIGO. ¿Dónde está?
>
>   ...
>
>   Señor, esto es perdición:
>   ella toma una naranja
>   y se come tres pepitas,
>   y yo ando siempre a la cuarta. (Jornada 2)

> ROSA. I only eat what I absolutely need, I don't need the rest.
> BODIGO. But I am in need of it, servants usually get tired of that which is left over from their masters but poor Bodigo goes around always gnawing at his own name, because nothing is ever left over.
> ROSA. You can eat whatever you want.
> BODIGO. Where is it? ... Sir, this is eternal condemnation: she takes an orange and eats three quarters and I end up always with the fourth.

Again Bodigo references his own name as a reminder of the food he does not eat. One-fourth of an orange is nothing for one who is so hungry, and so much so that he constantly refers to eating himself. This use of Bodigo's name to refer to the sacramental food, while at the same time evoking images of self-cannibalism, is another instance in which the authors mesh together stereotypes of the two traditions, Catholic and Indigenous. Thus, while Bodigo serves as comic relief, he also reminds the audience of the dangers lurking just beneath the surface. This reference is also reminiscent of Pinelo's warning to the readers of *Questión moral*, which linked human flesh to chocolate as a deterrent to incorporating any Indigenous traditions into Catholic practices.

The play ends with Rosa saving both Lima and Juan from falling to the devil's desires. Her death is brought on from her great efforts to save everyone from the devil and the Indigenous army that has advanced on Lima, which prove to be especially difficult in her already weakened state. Both her potential suitor, Juan, and her hapless servant, Bodigo, promise to join the Dominican order in her honour, thus indicating the salvation of the Americas and their subjugation to Catholicism. Bodigo, for all his base desires and potential barbarity, has been converted, and the dangers of the New World are subdued. In spite of Pinelo's cautionary measures, *Santa Rosa del Perú* shows the Spanish audience a New World that is slowly becoming incorporated into the Old World religion – now with its very own patron saint – while maintaining some of its own, select traditions, traditions that are bleeding across the Atlantic and permeating Spanish society. The mixture will birth the baroque understanding of the world, a world that is forever changed by the often violent confrontation of these two disparate spaces. Plays such as *Santa Rosa* bring the unfamiliar home for the audience. Chocolate, once seen as an erotic and powerful symbol of the Aztecs, is now "a symbol of the consumption of the colonized Self" (Gamboa 25). Eventually, chocolate is relegated to the Catholic faith; if Rosa can drink it medicinally during her fast and still become the saviour of Lima and bride of Christ in death, then it is safe for the Spanish public, with whom it has been growing in popularity in spite of the ecclesiastical debates that surround its worth.

Chocolate, therefore, is somewhere in the space between: a symbol of Otherness, barbarity, as described by Pinelo; and Self – or at least an acceptable substitute for those things that we claim as our own – as shown by Hurtado. Yolanda Gamboa claims that in *Santa Rosa* chocolate actually becomes a cultural object that props up Spain's national identity, even as its empire begins to crumble:

> It helped Spain stand out in the European scene for a century, until the discovery of the chocolate recipe that parallels the progressive decay of the Spanish Empire. Both a metaphor for the Self [the consumer] and stereotype of the colonized Other [the consumed] chocolate, thus, contributes to the definition of an identity established against the cultural and ethnic Other, the colonial subject, as well as the social Other. Not surprisingly, the exoticized and eroticized Other from the colony slides in the seventeenth century to what is perceived as the problematic Other at home, namely, Woman. Women's association with chocolate in a Spain on the wane, serves to strengthen a cultural identity which is civilized and in control of its Others. (36)

Thus has a thoroughly baroque and transatlantic object been relegated to a sphere that can be easily controlled. For all of Pinelo's worry and Hurtado's mollification, chocolate appears to be a non-issue, one that can be incorporated into daily life in Spain because it – and its users – can be contained and manipulated to show, ultimately, that the Spanish Empire is still in control of its people and products. Roberto González-Echevarría maintains that "The Baroque allowed for a break with the Greco-Latin tradition by allowing the fringes, the frills, as it were, to proliferate, upsetting the balance of symmetry, displacing the centrality of renaissance aesthetics, and occupying an important position. Through its capaciousness and proliferation the Baroque inscribed the American" (198). What the Baroque does not allow for, however, is for the American to inscribe Spain. Instead, the Old World authors of the Baroque must find ways for the American to become Spanish, without usurping any of Spain's power. Thus, Hurtado's understanding of chocolate, as something always-already a part of the culture, allows for Spain to consider chocolate its own, without concerning itself overly with questions of provenance. Likewise, the Lanini y Sagredo act of *Santa Rosa* ignores the Indigenous use of chocolate and, as Gascón explains, "assesses its utility according to European beliefs" (47) by relegating its properties to the medicinal and spiritual. Both of these function within the baroque to blur the line between Other and Same, allowing the two to bleed into each other until they are almost indistinguishable, while still maintaining Old World superiority over the Other.

CHAPTER 5

Chocolate: A Prescription for Health?

While the religious debates were concerned mainly with the spiritual consequences of the consumption of chocolate, discussions of the medicinal effects were much more concerned with the corporeal ones. Even so, there were definitely overlaps in the two debates, and the religious debate had long-lasting ramifications in the medical community's perspective on chocolate. This makes sense, as Catholicism can and should be considered one of the most important cultural influences in early modern Spain, but the debates regarding chocolate's worth quickly extended beyond the religious and ventured into more scientific territory. The prevailing medical theory of the time concerned the "humours," four temperaments that were linked to heat and cold, humidity and dryness. Early modern medicine thus was concerned with balancing the humours, and treatments such as phlebotomizing or applying heat or cold to certain parts of the body were derived from the Hippocratic theory of the four humours. The arrival of chocolate in Spain, and its purported medicinal properties,[1] required practitioners and theorists of medicine to incorporate it into the humour classifications, although they often disagreed as to who would benefit from the use of chocolate, the amount that should be used, and its overall effects on the human body. These disagreements and contradictions continued well into the eighteenth century in the medical treatises.[2]

On the other hand, the literary sources had a more or less steady trajectory towards acceptance and promotion of the medicinal qualities of chocolate, as we will see. The reason for this may well be that the literature more clearly reflected societal acceptance of chocolate and the impetus to create a political and social environment that was favourable to the quickly spreading use – and some might even say abuse – of the transatlantic drink.

Religion influenced the early medical treatises as well as literary sources, as was the case with Bartolomé Marradón's fictionalized conversation *Diálogo del uso del tabaco, los daños y provechos que el tiempo y experiencia en descubierto de sus efectos, y del chocolate y otras bebidas que en estos tiempos se usan* (1618).[3] Marradón himself was a doctor from the small town of Marchena near Seville, and he wrote at least one other "Dialogue" regarding medicinal treatments. In the *Diálogo del uso* three archetypal characters engage in a conversation which is mostly disparaging of the idea of chocolate not only as a medicine but also generally:

MED. Je l'ay veu & goûté, mais pour vous dire la verité, il ne me plaist point ni pour breuvage, ni pour monnoye quelque loüange qu'on lui puisse donner. J'en ay oüy faire grand estat à un Medicin de nom & de reputation tant pour le gain qu'il retiroit de la composition de ce breuvage qu'on a de coûtume de faire venir en forme de petites tablettes ou de conserve; que pour la grande experience qu'il a de ses effects, qui l'obligent méme à donner à ses malades. Quant à la qualité des *Cacaos*, bien que pour servir à faire ce breuvage ils doivent etre cueillis un peu verdelets; si est-ce qu'on a de coûtume de choisir les plus secs & les plus vieux; & nonobstant cela ils ne laissent pas d'avoir un goust âpre, adstringent & si desagreable, qu'il n'est pas de merveille si ceux qui en goustent, ont en horreur le breuvage qu'on en fait. (169–70)

DOCTOR. I have seen and tasted it, but to tell you the truth, I don't like the praise some lavish on it, neither as a beverage, or as currency. I hear a

Doctor of good name and reputation make much ado about it; so much is the benefit he draws from the composition of this beverage, which usually comes in the form of little bars or as a preserve, that due to the positive experience he obtains from its effects, he is even obliged to give it to his sick patients. As for the quality of the Cacaos, when used to make this beverage they must be picked while still a bit green; if one is accustomed to selecting the driest and oldest beans, and notwithstanding it still has a bitter, astringent, and disagreeable taste, well, it is no wonder if those who taste it are horrified by the beverage it makes. (Trans. Pupillo)

While the Doctor is aware that there are other medical practitioners who use this newly encountered drink, he himself remains unconvinced. To further underline this point, an Indigenous character also disparages the drink, replying "Je me ris de ceux qui disent que ce breuvage refraîchit, & qu'il est grandement medicinal, soit qu'on le prenne dissout en eau tiede, soit qu'on le prenne épais comme de la viande à manger" ("I laugh at those who say that this beverage is refreshing, and that it is highly medicinal, whether taken dissolved in warm water, or thickened like meat to eat"; 171; trans. Pupillo). By placing the denigrating remarks in the mouth of an Indigenous character, Marradón lends authority to the disregard in which the Doctor holds chocolate and its users. If the Indigenous community is not using chocolate medicinally, then why should Spain? After all, it is Indigenous inhabitants of the New World who have cultivated and ingested chocolate for centuries prior to the arrival of Spaniards – if they have reaped no demonstrable benefit from it and denigrate the claims of those who do, then it must not be useful pharmaceutically.

The dialogue shifts and connects itself back to the religious debate when the Indigenous character notes that there are even priests who are addicted to the drink:

IND. J'ai veu méme en un port de mer où nous debarquames pour puiser de l'eau un Prestre que nous disant la Messe comme un Apôtre, fut

obligé par necessité estant fort gras & fort fatigué de s'affeoir sur un
banc devant l'action de graces qu'on fait apre la Communion où estoit
une servante qui tennoit un vaisseau de *Thecomate* plain de *Chocolate*
qu'il beaut & Diue liu donna les forces d'achever la Messe apres s'estre
reposé. (181)

INDIAN. I have even seen, in a seaport where we disembarked to get
water, a Priest who, while saying Mass like an Apostle, was obliged
by necessity, being quite fat and tired, to sit down on a bench before
saying grace, which one does to start Communion, where there was
a servant who held a *Thecomate* vessel full of Chocolate, which the
priest drank, and with it God gave him the strength to finish the Mass
after he had rested. (Trans. Pupillo)

He is ultimately pardoned by the Doctor because he is afflicted by an
"infirmity"; the Doctor also reminds his listeners that anyone who is
not ill must refrain from such indulgences, even though the bourgeois
character notes the prevalent use of chocolate in colonial Masses,
demonstrating its widespread consumption. Although the Doctor figures prominently in the dialogue – understandably, given Marradón's
own connection to the profession – there is no real medical advice
dispensed regarding the drinking of chocolate, other than to equate it
to tobacco and advocate for restricted usage.

   The connection between religion and science on this matter persists
well into the eighteenth century. In 1754 a priest, Fray José Vicente
Díaz Bravo, published a book on the reformed rules for fasting in the
Church which he subtitled *Obra historica, canonico-medica, necesaria
a los señores Obispos, curas confesores, medicos, sanos y enfermos*.
If all this were not already a tall order, he also promises a specific dissertation on the history, medicine, chemistry, physicality, and moral-
ity of chocolate and its uses at the end of the book. As a priest, Díaz
Bravo makes the connection between religion and medicine, as he
claims that in order for the theologian to understand the place of
chocolate within the Church, either inside or outside of fasting, one

must also understand its properties: "cómo averiguará el teólogo, si el chocolate quebranta, o no el ayuno, sin saber primero la substancia, y nutrimento, que da de sí el cacao? Esto no lo puede el teólogo saber, sin la química y física experimental: con que sin el auxilio de estas, no puede arribar en este asunto, ni toda la teología" ("how will the theologian figure out if chocolate breaks the fast or not, without first knowing the substance and nutrition that chocolate itself can give? The theologian cannot know this, without physical and chemical experiments: for without the help of those things, he cannot come to a conclusion in this matter, nor can all of theology"; 314). Díaz Bravo mixes religious and medicinal treatises to make his point, resolving that "El chocolate del modo, que hoy se usa en España, es rigurosamente comida. Pudiera citar para este asunto innumerables Teólogos, y Médicos, pero me contento con unos pocos pero de mucha nota" ("Chocolate, in the mode in which it is used today, is obviously food. I could cite innumerable theologians and doctors on this issue, but I will be contented with just a few, of high esteem"; 318). Díaz Bravo goes on to name these famed theologians and doctors and cites the conclusions that favour his own.

Among those considered worthy of inclusion we find Marco Mappo, whose 1695 treatise concludes that chocolate is a mass that can be mixed with a variety of other ingredients and is fairly healthy, but is best considered a food that can help recuperate health (qtd by Díaz Bravo 318); Díaz Bravo also cites an experiment by the physician Juan Royo that demonstrates that chocolate is a primarily fatty substance, thus proving his own hypothesis that chocolate is more food than drink (315). Finally, he mentions the Italian doctor Geronimo Piperi, whose comments on the poem "Décima glosada al chocolate," which was reprinted and glossed throughout the eighteenth century, also make the religion-medicine connection. The original "Décima," without Piperi's notes, can be found in Thomas Cortijo Herraiz's 1729 *Discurso apologético médico astronómico*:

Es rocío celestial:
Cifra de todo alimento;
Conservación, y aún aumento
De el húmido radical.
Néctar precioso y vital,
Medicina de los males,
Y en fin, de virtudes tales,
que si acaso le bebieron
a su eficacia debieron
ser los Dioses inmortales. (Qtd by Cortijo Herraiz 116)[4]

It is a celestial dew: key of all food; conservation and even augmentation
of the lymphatic humour. Precious and vital nectar, medicine of illnesses,
and, finally, of so many virtues, that if they happened to drink it, with its
efficacy the Gods should be immortal.

It is Piperi's notes in the glossed version, however, that pointedly make
the connection between the sciences of chocolate and spirituality. The
glossed version has a total of one hundred lines, ten in each stanza,
the tenth of each being a line from the original poem. The first line in
the unglossed version, "Es rocío celestial," already indicates the connection to the heavens, and the stanza dedicated to that line draws
out the association, including lines such as "Tiene cierta vecindad, / A
el orden espiritual" ("It has a certain affinity to the spiritual order";
116). It is the explication of the third line, "Conservación y aun
aumento," however, that starts to bring in the possible health benefits:

Es quien prolonga las vidas,
Pues es su virtud sagaz,
La que establece la paz
En cualidades reñidas;
Las suyas son tan subidas,
Y de tal temperamento,

Que a todo el humano aliento
Lo vuelve a su edad temprana,
Siendo la vida humana
Conservación y aun aumento. (117, emphasis in the original)

It is what prolongs lives, such is its prudent virtue, that which establishes peace in opposing qualities; its own are so elevated, and of such a temperament, that it returns all human spirit to a younger age, being to human life conservation and even augmentation.

Chocolate is therefore posed as the elixir or fountain of youth, not only prolonging lives but also turning back time – making connections not only to the spiritual world, as in the first stanza, but also to some kind of otherworldly or magical realm.[5]

Piperi's "Décima glosada" also makes reference to the prevalent medical conception of human health and wellness of the time: the four humours or temperaments that originated from the writings of Hippocrates. The proto-medical theory behind the humours stated that there were four predominant bodily fluids, and their balance – or lack thereof – in the human body would lend a certain personality to each individual. These humours – sanguine, choleric, melancholic, and phlegmatic – were each tied to personality traits and were also classified according to certain elements – hot, cold, wet, and dry – and it was the excess tendency towards two of these that would indicate a person's connection to one of the humours. Elements outside the human body, such as food, were also considered along the hot/cold, wet/dry spectrum and were prescribed in varying quantities to each individual according to what they were seen as lacking, so as to try and balance out the humours. Cortijo Herraiz claims that "no se puede asignar regla general sobre el asunto … que las reglas generales se parecían mucho a las mujeres, en que las más veces engañaban" ("one cannot assign a general rule here … as general rules are very much like women, in that, more often than not, they fool you";

103). He is willing to state that, for the most part, those of a choleric humour should drink cold water before and after chocolate, since it will absorb any excesses that might be mixed therein and be harmful to those with such a temperament. Those with a phlegmatic disposition, on the other hand, are advised not to drink anything before chocolate, as doing so will weaken their stomachs (103). As with most other comestibles, Cortijo Herraiz errs on the side of caution, believing that those of different temperaments should take care not to upset the humours by ingesting something in a way not prescribed. In fact, he goes so far as to say that he truly does not wish to make a rule at all, because he has observed so many differing reactions: "Protesto ante todas cosas, que no es mi animo el establecer por regla general, ni por precepto perpetuo el uso del chocolate en las enfermedades; pues habiendo notado la diversidad de los efectos, que ocasiona en los sanos, por la diferente disposición de cada individuo" ("I protest, above all, that it is not in my nature to establish general rules, nor a permanent order to use chocolate in illnesses; having noted the diversity of the effects that it can bring on in those who are healthy, according to the varying disposition of each individual"; 106–7).

Still, even if Cortijo Herraiz is unwilling to set anything in stone, there are other medical practitioners who are. Santiago Valverde Turices wrote one of the early discourses dedicated solely to chocolate, published over a century before Cortijo Herraiz's *Discurso* in Seville, in 1625. In his book he directly responds to the question of whose temperament is better suited to chocolate, and for whom is it worse. He bases his response on the idea that "el chocolate es caliente, húmedo, untuoso: y con facilidad se vuelve en cólera ... que no tenía naturaleza de tierra, o agua, sino de aire, o fuego: y también el chocolate tiene partes calientes y secas, que alteraran mas el colérico que el flemático" ("chocolate is hot, humid and greasy: and with ease it turns into choler ... it has no nature of the earth or water, but rather air, or fire: and it also has hot and dry parts, that affect the choleric nature more than the phlegmatic"; C4). He concludes that, given the nature of chocolate, it is most problematic for melancholic humours, followed by phlegmatic, then sanguine, and finally choleric.

Antonio Colmenero de Ledesma's *Curioso tratado de la naturaleza y calidad del chocolate* appears shortly after Valverde's treatise, in 1631, and is divided into four parts: the first, discussing what chocolate is, and the quality of cacao and other ingredients; the second, examining the quality of chocolate as a whole; the third, considering the different ways to make and drink chocolate in the Indies, and which of those is most healthy; and finally, the fourth, discussing the quantity and manner in which it should be drunk, as well as when, and by whom. In his opening letter to the reader, Colmenero asserts that he has not seen any other writings regarding the medical properties of chocolate save for those by an unnamed doctor from Marchena – a small town in the province of Seville – who was so incorrect in his judgment of chocolate's uses and effects that Colmenero feels he must set the record straight (1r).[6]

It is not until the third section of the book that Colmenero explains how to make a chocolate that any good, healthy person can partake in, while those with afflictions should add or remove ingredients to suit their needs. His recipe incorporates many New World ingredients and techniques, while also attempting to give some Spanish substitutes where possible (see Appendix 1 for ingredient list). He then lists a number of methods of preparation, including those used originally by the Indigenous peoples and those invented to suit the Spaniards' tastes. Here he interjects his medical opinion on the different methods, of which the use of extra butter and fats is the most critiqued: "no lo tengo por tan saludable, si bien más gustoso, porque como se aparta la manteca de lo terrestre, que queda abajo, esto causa melancolía, y la manteca relaja el estómago, y quita la gana de comer" ("I do not find this one as healthy, even if more delicious, because the manner in which the butter is separated from the rest, which remains below, can cause melancholy, and the butter relaxes the stomach, and cuts the appetite"; 9v). Thus, just as the religious debates were concerned with the nutritive properties of chocolate, and the possibility it had to break the fast, here we see with our first medical treatise the same concern, that certain recipes might, indeed, be too filling to be healthy. The method he most recommends and uses himself is one that he says is for "businessmen," as it is the quickest, least heavy recipe. It seems, however, also to be the least interesting, containing only hot water, chocolate, and sugar (10r).

Colmenero de Ledesma is most concerned about temperament in the fourth section, which covers the quantity that one drinks, and the time of year; specifying that those in Spain who are unaccustomed to the drink should avoid it particularly in the hotter part of the year, even though it is customary to drink it throughout the year in the Indies (10v). He also reminds the reader that the addition of fatty ingredients is part of what makes chocolate truly unhealthy:

Con todo digo, que las muchas partes mantecosas ... son las que impinguan,[7] y engordan, y las calientes que entran en esta composición, le sirven de guía y vehículo, para que pasan por el hígado, y las demás partes, hasta llegar a las carnosas, y allí como hallan sustancia símil, que es caliente y húmeda, como lo es la mantecosa, convirtiéndose en sustancia del sujeto, lo aumenta, e impingua. (11r)

With all I say, that the many fatty parts ... which are those that enrich and fatten and the heat that enters in this composition, should serve as their guide and vehicle, so that they pass through the liver, and other parts, until they reach the fleshier ones, and there they will find similar sustenance, which is hot and humid, as is the grease, which, converting itself into sustenance for the person, will increase and fatten him up.

Thus, the religious debate on whether or not chocolate gives enough nutrients to sustain someone who is fasting appears similarly in the medical debates as the recognition that too much of a good thing could actually cause the imbiber to gain weight.

Although the literature does not delve deep into the effects on varying temperaments, Juan de la Mata's cookbook, *Arte de repostería* (1747), does make note of the medicinal uses of chocolate, which are also presented in various literary works: "Es utilísimo hecho con la debida puridad para confortar el estomago, y el pecho; mantiene, y restablece el calor natural; alimenta, disipa, y destruye los humores malignos; fortifica, y sustenta la voz" ("It is very useful if made with the necessary purity, to comfort the stomach and chest; it maintains and re-establishes natural warmth; it nourishes, clears and destroys malignant humours; it fortifies and sustains the voice"; 145). This same book includes a recipe similar to Colmenero de Ledesma's for the businessman, but that additionally allows for the inclusion of cinnamon. Mata claims that the French are particularly fond of this mixture for its health benefits and that they call it *"chocolat de santé"* ("healthy chocolate"; 145, emphasis in the original).

In spite of these claims of chocolate's powers to heal all ills, there are also counterclaims that argue that there are varying degrees of "goodness" or "badness" to chocolate, particularly when it comes to purity and/or the mixing of other ingredients into the drink. The rapid integration of chocolate into Spanish society left open many questions regarding its use, value, and potential problems. In 1666, the Order of Doctors of Madrid advised the King and his councillors – which would include Mariana de Austria, King Charles II's mother and Queen Regent – on chocolate, warning them that the greed of those who sell chocolate could pose a public health problem with their use of low-quality ingredients, and blaming these sellers for a rash of recent diseases and even some unexpected and potentially avoidable deaths ("Consulta Original de Los Médicos de Orden de Madrid Sobre El Chocolate" 284). To counteract these issues, they recommend that the court study the quality and variety of chocolate and restrict prices – "pues no siendo todo de una calidad y perfección, no se deben promiscuamente igualar en los precios" ("since it is not all of the same quality and perfection, one should not allow them to be indiscriminately equal in price"; "Consulta original de los médicos de orden de Madrid sobre el chocolate" 284–5) – and likewise regulate the ingredients, both in terms of quality and the individual components themselves: "que en el chocolate no se debe permitir (el maíz ni bellote) por la suma astricción, de donde es cierto se deben temer grandes enfermidades" ("that in chocolate it should not be permitted even in the smallest quantity (neither maize nor acorn), for that is from where it is certain that great illness should be feared"; 285). The fears of many of the doctors writing about chocolate at the time are similar: it is not necessarily the chocolate itself that causes harm, but rather the ingredients being added for flavour and pleasure, and the quantities being consumed. Published only three years before the decree, *Día y noche de Madrid* by Francisco Santos also makes note of the problems caused by adding ingredients, particularly for those of a more "delicate character":

Es un barrio el que habita de gente delicada, destos que se visten con luz sin salir de la cama, muy cerradas las ventanas por que no entre aire, y si toman chocolate y tiene a su parecer más azúcar de lo que ha menester, dicen que es húmeda y los ha hecho mal; otras veces dicen que está muy tostado el cacao; otras, que la canela era fuerte; otras veces dicen que el pimiento los mata y luego llaman al médico ... (704)

It is a neighbourhood inhabited by delicate folks, those ones that get dressed by lamplight without even leaving their bed, with their windows shut tight to keep the air out, and if they drink chocolate, and it has, in their opinion, more sugar than it should, they say it's humid and has made them sick; other times they say that the cacao is too burnt; others, that the cinnamon is too strong; and other times they say that the pepper is killing them and they call straight for the doctor ...

By disparaging the "delicate" nature of those who complain about their chocolate, this character, we can infer, thinks little of the upper class who have to get dressed while still in bed, cannot breathe fresh air, and always find some way to complain about how the chocolate is made. Clearly, he has little regard for the idea that any of these issues would cause death, or even illness.

Moderation in ingredients and consumption is a theme repeated throughout the medical texts of the time. Even prior to the Order of Doctors' recommendations to the King and Colmenero's concerns over weight gain, Valverde Turices notes that, although other doctors writing from the other side of the Atlantic, such as Juan de Barrios – whose *Libro en el cual se trata del chocolate, que provechos haga y si es bebida saludable o no* (1609) was first printed in Mexico[8] – have suggested certain recipes, such mixtures are problematic:

> ... hay dominio en algunos, y aparecen las calidades, y virtudes, o daños de los que dominan, y por eso quitaré la pimienta de Chiapa, por que mueven lujuria, las vainillas, y mecaxochitl, porque siendo tan movedores de orina, y meses, y aceleran el parto, y hacen echar la criatura muerta, no la hagan echar sin tiempo viva, o causen enfermedad de orina a quien estuviere apercibido a ella, o flujo de meses a quien le bebiere estando con la visita. (A3v)

> ... there is power in some [of the ingredients], and the qualities, virtues, or harmful qualities that control the ingredients can take over, and for that reason I would remove the Chiapan pepper, because it causes lust; the vanillas and mecaxochitl [a plant related to black pepper], because they provoke urine, and menstruation, and accelerate childbirth, which in turn causes stillbirths ... or causes urinary infections in those who are prone to them, or an overflowing of menses in those who drink it during their time of the month.

That is not to say that it is impossible to drink chocolate mixed with other ingredients. Valverde Turices provides two recipes: one for the Indies and one for when the imbiber must find substitutes as they are unable to access goods from the New World. Cárdenas provides a possible explanation for why some ingredients are considered perfectly fine on one side of the Atlantic but not on the other. His premise – to which he devotes approximately one-third of *Problemas y secretos maravillosos* – is that those Europeans who are born in the New World, or spend a large portion of their life there, are physically different from their counterparts who grow up on the Continent. He argues that it is the humid climate of the Indies that promotes changes in not only their physical being but also their quality of life, claiming that exposure to the climate of the Indies both ages people more rapidly and raises their intellect. Although Indigenous peoples are also exposed to this climate, it affects them differently, according to his reasoning, since they already have the proper humours adapted to the humidity (179v–180r and 183r–184v).

Valverde seems to have a particular interest in the issues that arise from women's consumption of chocolate. He wants to remove not only the additions that might provoke lust but also those that might damage a woman's health during menstruation and pregnancy (his concern for the latter being more with the child and the potential for stillbirth). The connection between chocolate and childbirth makes its literary debut in Luis Quiñones de Benavente's *Entremés de la constreñida* (1657):[9]

> PEDRO. Hallándose mi hermana en tal aprieto
> determinose consultar al punto
> los Médicos mejores de Torrijos,
> adonde es discreción hacer sus hijos
>
> …
>
> De aqueste aborto mi hermana tuvo un niño,
> y diole luego usagre, y almorranas;
> mas no se le quitaron las cuartanas,
> aunque tomó tabaco, y chocolate;
> al seteno la fiebre dio remate

al humor grueso, y el Doctor Salgado
avisó de secreto, que era hurtado,
y le dieron la Unción. (15v)

PEDRO. My sister, finding herself in such a state, was determined to consult
immediately with the best doctors of Torrijos, where it is prudent
to have children ... From that labour my sister had a boy who later
developed impetigo and piles, but they could not rid him of the fever,
even though he took tobacco and chocolate; and on the seventh day
the fever finished off with black humour, and Doctor Salgado advised
privately that he was gone, and they administered the Extreme Unction.

Given that the original medical advice dispensed by Valverde warns
that giving a pregnant woman chocolate could potentially contribute
to a stillbirth, it seems odd that the newborn child is given both chocolate and tobacco – the latter of which for the modern reader seems even
more anomalous as a medicine[10] – but since the *entremés* genre itself is
not known for being overly precise or realistic, but rather comical and
satirical, the accuracy of the content cannot be presumed. It is almost
impossible to guess what the meaning behind this scene was, as it is
not elaborated and the entire *entremés* is just a series of disconnected
stories about the sister of the main character and her various exploits,
but perhaps the mixture of tobacco and chocolate is partially to blame,
which would reinforce the medical advice of the day; that is, to keep
the chocolate recipes simple, as Colmenero has suggested.[11]

Returning to Piperi's "Décima glosada al chocolate," which generally indicates that chocolate is a universal medicine that can cure just
about any ill and prolong life, we still find some qualifying statements.
The ninth stanza, in particular, is also reflected by Fr. Alonso Barbadillo, one of the censors of Cortijo Herraiz's *Discurso apologético
médico astronómico*, the very same book that the "Décima glosada"
appears in: "Si es bueno; bueno. Si es malo; malo" ("If it is good;
good. If it is bad; bad." "Aprobación" n.p.):

No hay cosa mejor, si es bueno,
Ni cosa peor, si es malo;
Es triaca, si está ralo,
Y si está espeso, es veneno;
De todo extremo es ajeno,
Pues por él unos murieron,
Y por él otros vivieron,
Con salud robusta, ufanos,
Y el vivir siempre tan sanos
A *su eficacia debieron*. ("Décima glosada" 119, emphasis in the original)

There is nothing better, if it is good, nor worse, if it is bad; it is an antidote, if it is runny, and if thick, a poison; and it varies from one extreme to the other, as some die because of it, and others live, with robust health, satisfied, and living healthy can be attributed to its efficacy.

In spite of these efforts in both the medicinal treatises and the literature to warn of the potential dangers of excessive use of chocolate, particularly that which is not kept in a pure state, the prevailing public opinion seems to favour the use of chocolate as a cure-all. In a 1669 recommendation on commerce and tariffs to Mariana de Austria, the city council of Madrid notes:

El chocolate es alimento tan necesario, como el pan, vino, y carne, y se ha hecho tan común, que no hay ninguna persona, desde el más alto al más bajo estado, que no le use, no por la golosina, sino preciso para la salud, como se puede discurrir del mucho consumo; y si sobre el precio tan alto a que ahora vale el cacao, que es el ingrediente principal, se cargan de los 5 por 100 se imposibilitará, que muchas personas, que casi se sustentan con solo chocolate, no lo puedan comprar, ocasionándose muchas enfermedades. (López and Pérez de Herrera 173v)

Chocolate is so necessary a food, like bread, wine, and meat, and it has become so common, that there is no one, from the highest to the lowest stature, that does not use it, not because of the taste, but rather for their health, as can be derived from the high rate of consumption; and if, on top of the high price at which cacao is currently valued, being the principal ingredient, they are charged 5 per cent, it will become impossible for many people, who practically sustain themselves with chocolate alone, to purchase it, which will in turn cause many illnesses.

The councillors are far less concerned with the effects of excess than with the potential for withdrawal that a 5 per cent tax might cause for those who have come to view chocolate as a part of the most basic of early modern diets. The forewarning of the council of Madrid is in line with the idea that chocolate is a healthy cure-all that can and should be consumed at all times. Not all doctors, however, agreed that this was a course to be followed by all, with many erring on the side of moderation, and some even calling for chocolate to be avoided by everyone, ill or well.

On the side of moderation, Valverde calls for imbibers to limit themselves to certain times of day, mainly the morning, as drinking chocolate in the late afternoon or night time can cause insomnia and inflammation of the throat (C3v), while, as previously noted, Colmenero insists that it should be avoided for entire seasons. There are similar warnings in the literary sources. The Doctor, for example, in Marradón's *Dialogue* also warns that giving it at any time of the day to all people, regardless of age or gender, should be avoided, a warning akin to those he has already given on tobacco (180). Even the "Décima glosada," which first lauds chocolate as a cure-all, ends with a warning on the dangers of overuse:

Quien le sabe usar, es raro:
No le tomes muy espeso,
Ni tampoco con exceso,
Porque suele costar caro. (119)

He who knows how to use it is rare: Do not take it thick, or with excess, because it can cost you dearly.

Still, the overarching argument of the "Décima," in both the original and glossed versions, is that he who knows the secrets of chocolate can use it to cure all ills, maintain health, and perhaps even become immortal. The added expository lines in the first eight out of the ten stanzas are pure acclamation, while the last two do add some conditions to help guide the user. The ninth, cited earlier, mentions the possibility of chocolate turning to poison if too thick, while the tenth and final stanza, above, does promise great cost for those who drink it to excess, but also concludes that those who use it well will live healthily and that it is to this treasure that the gods owe their immortality (119), hardly a heavy-handed condemnation such as can be found in the medical texts.

Carolyn Nadeau's exhaustive study on the food practices of early modern Spain also points to bread, wine, and meat as central to the seventeenth-century diet (see pages 7, 42, and 46 respectively). Given that Nadeau takes her cue from the opening passage of Cervantes' first volume of the *Quixote*, originally published in 1605, the recommendation quoted above demonstrates that in little more than a half-century chocolate has gained a status on par with the most important and basic components on the table. This is corroborated by the famous French travel diary, *Mémoires de la cour d'Espagne* (1677), compiled by Marie Catherine le Jumel de Barneville, better known as Madame d'Aulnoy. She explains that, upon arriving at the house of the princess, they were invited to join her and her entourage for a snack, at which they were served a variety of chocolates and other sweets:

Presentaron después el chocolate, cada taza de porcelana sobre un platito de ágata, guarnecido de oro, con azúcar en una caja de lo mismo. Había allí chocolate helado, otro caliente y otro con leche y huevos. Lo toman con bizcochos o panecillos tan secos como si estuviesen fritos, y los hacen expresamente. Hay señoras que toman de todo y unas tazas tras otras seguidas, y a menudo dos y tres veces al día, lo que hay que sorprenderse de que estén tan secas, puesto que nada hay más caliente, y además de eso, comen todo con tanta pimienta y tantas especias, que es imposible el que no se tuesten; habían varias que comían trozos de *arcilla sigelada*. (qtd by Díez Borque 100, emphasis in the original)

They then presented the chocolate, each porcelain cup on a little plate of quartz, adorned with gold, with sugar in a box made of the same materials. There was frozen chocolate, another hot, and another with milk and eggs. They drink it with biscuits or little bread rolls, so dry that you'd think they were fried, and they make them just for that purpose. There are women who drink all of them, and one after another, and often two or three times a day, and it is surprising that they're all so dry, given that there is nothing hotter, and on top of that, they eat it all with so much pepper and other spices, that it seems impossible that they don't roast themselves; there were also many women that ate *clay dirt*.

It would appear that Madame d'Aulnoy subscribes to the medical opinion of the day, that the ingestion of so "hot" a food would cause a similar reaction within the body of the imbiber. Still, her assertion that it has become customary to drink chocolate regularly, up to three times a day, and several cups at a time, indicates its popularity at the time of her visit during the second half of the seventeenth century. Of course, her comments towards the end of the passage regarding the women's overindulgence and the potential health risks, coupled with the odd addition about the ingestion of clay, might indicate that d'Aulnoy was not much of a fan of the eating habits of Spanish women.

The appearance of a *baile* (danced interlude) named *Baile del chocolatero* in the late seventeenth century also demonstrates the high level of interest and recognition that the product had gained by that time. We cannot be sure of the authorship or exact date of the work, as we are given only the following information on the title page of the anthology in which it appears: "Estos sainetes son de los dos mejores ingenious de España Don Pedro Calderón y Don Agustín Moreto, los que no se han impreso, porque lo rehusaron sus autores" ("These farces are from the two greatest geniuses of Spain, Don Pedro Calderón and Don Agustín Moreto, and have not been printed before, because their authors refused to do so"; *Colección de bailes, mojigangas, entremeses y coplas*). And even that information is doubtful, as many of these plays and interludes have since been attributed to a variety of other authors. In spite of the lack of recognition by the authors themselves and the lack of attribution within the text, the *Baile del chocolatero* is the only theatrical piece, interlude or full length, that is specifically dedicated to chocolate and chocolate production in its entirety. With only five, unnamed characters, two women and two men, plus the titular chocolate maker, this short interlude touches on almost every aspect of chocolate discussed thus far, including the economics, religious implications, and, of course, potential medical uses.[12] The latter, the most pertinent to the purposes of this chapter, is discussed thus:

1°. Señor, aunque el chocolate
    tomo, no me hace provecho,
    porque es un fuego en verano,
    y es muy caliente en invierno,
    y aun quisiera saber
    ¿para que achaques es bueno?
CHOCOLATERO. Ya que me lo ha preguntado
    yo se lo diré bien presto. (199)

FIRST MAN. Sir, although I drink chocolate, it does me no good, because
    it is like fire in the summer and very hot in the winter, and thus I
    wanted to know, for which ailments is it good?
CHOCOLATIER. Now that you have asked me, I will tell you forthwith.

Although he is asked and promises to provide the information, he instead pivots to the use of chocolate during fasting, giving no real insight into the medicinal properties of the drink. Given the general satirical and somewhat ridiculous nature of the short interludes, and the chocolatier's obvious desire to sell chocolate to his interlocutors, there are two possible reasons for this rapid change of topic. For one, it could just be that the author found it unnecessary, given that there is little plot to any of the *entremeses* and the nature of the genre does not require any real congruity. The other, perhaps more coherent reason for the conversational turn may be that the chocolatier knows that there are no tangible benefits to chocolate and wishes to avoid any buyer's remorse coming back to haunt him later on.

Whether or not any chocolate seller knew for certain that there were any real medicinal benefits, allowing the sick to ingest chocolate medicinally was still promoted in both treatises and literary texts. The arguments for it are threefold: first, it can revitalize and restore appetite as well as satiate hunger and thirst; second, it can calm an uneasy stomach; and third, it can pacify aggravations of the chest and lungs. This last claim is reflected in the anonymous interlude *Entremés del nigromántico* (1685), in which the protagonist, Lorenzo, claims that chocolate is too hot for his "livianos" or inflamed lungs: "Señora hermosa, yo estoy / de los livianos enfermo, / y me enciende el chocolate" ("Beautiful señora, I am afflicted with enflamed lungs, and chocolate sets them on fire"; *El nigromántico* 24). She insists, however, saying that she has added ingredients that will remove the heat of chocolate's composition: "Pues no lo dejéis por esto, / que con perejil le hice, / porque estuviese más fresco" ("Do not reject it for that reason; I made it with parsley, so that it would be more cooling"; 24). Although Lorenzo does not want to eat or drink what is put before him at first, he seems to be easily persuaded that with a little added parsley – an ingredient that you would not find in any of the regular recipes – chocolate will in fact do him some good.

The idea of chocolate as a salve for the stomach and satiation of hunger or thirst actually appears far more frequently in the literary sources than the medical treatises. As we saw in the previous chapter, in *Santa Rosa de Perú*, Rosa consents to take a small amount of chocolate to quell her stomach pain. One wonders if the pain that Rosa feels could just be attributed to hunger, since she has been fasting a long time and her servant pleads with her to eat anything:

ROSA. Mucho más es de notar
    mi miseria, que el dolor
    de estómago con rigor
    me comienza a fatigar.
BODIGO. Come algo, y ten buena maña,
    porque el dolor se mitigue.
ROSA. Ay, hermano, que prosigue
    con violencia muy extraña.
BODIGO. Come algo.
ROSA. Esto es tentación. (Jornada 2)

ROSA. My misery is much more notable than the rigorous stomach pain
    that begins to fatigue me.
BODIGO. Eat something, and be good about it, so that the pain might
    diminish quickly.
ROSA. Oh, brother, it proceeds with an extreme violence.
BODIGO. Eat something.
ROSA. This is temptation.

Although Rosa resists for much of the play, the pain becomes too much for her and when her father, Gaspar, insists that there must be some remedy, she finally consents to take a very small amount of chocolate, which her servant proclaims a "sánalo todo" ("cure-all"; jornada 3). Likewise, in *La fuerza del natural*, also written partially by Agustín Moreto and first appearing in the fifteenth part of *Comedias nuevas, escogidas de los mejores ingenios de España,* we find another *gracioso* whose main focus is on the base instincts.[13] Here, Julio, the *gracioso,* complains of hunger pains brought on by the late lunches in which the upper class partake:

> JULIO. Comamos, que rabio de hambre.
> AURORA. Si esta flaqueza sentís,
> haré que os traigan ahora
> chocolate.
> JULIO. ¿Qué señora?
> AURORA. Chocolate, ¿no lo oís?
> JULIO. ¿Cordellate? es uso importune,
> también allá lo gastamos,
> mas para calzas lo usamos
> más que para desayuno. (Moreto and Cáncer 1:11)

> JULIO. Let's eat, what hunger pains.
> AURORA. If such a weakness you feel, I'll make them bring you some
> chocolate right away.
> JULIO. What now, señora?
> AURORA. Chocolate, can't you hear?
> JULIO. Corduroy?[14] That's an odd use, we have it too, but we use it more
> for breeches than for breakfast.

Between this and *Santa Rosa,* written approximately eight years later, there is a large leap in Moreto's characters' understanding of the New World product. In *Santa Rosa* the *gracioso* is very aware of chocolate, its healing powers, and its flavour. *Santa Rosa* is also set in Lima, which might account for at least some of the disparity in the characters' reactions. Julio does not even seem to know the word, mistaking it for *cordellate,* or grosgrain, a completely inedible fabric, suggesting that, at least for the lower, servant class in Spain, chocolate is still not a household name.

Still, 1661 seems rather late for chocolate to remain unknown in Spanish society, and Santos's *Día y noche de Madrid*, which appeared only two years later than *La fuerza del natural*, contradicts the notion entirely. On the morning of the second day, a servant girl goes out in search of fuel to heat her lady's house and boil water for her morning chocolate. The first house she enters is so destitute that she completely forgets her task and returns home, recounting the misery she encountered. The lady of the house is moved by the empathy of her servant and promises to take care of the poor family from then on, with all the food they can eat. The reader never finds out exactly what food she sends them, only that she herself breakfasts on chocolate.

Nevertheless, seventeenth-century medical treatises focus mainly on the general "goodness" or "badness" of chocolate, and it is not until we move into the eighteenth century that we find specific mentions of the use of chocolate as a stomach balm. Cortijo Herraiz (1729) specifically calls chocolate "una bebida estomacal" ("a stomach drink") that is very smooth, given the high saturation of fats (111). He continues, claiming that it is "referativo de las obstrucciones, y cura las caquexias, a los Pthificos deplorados, los cura su cuotidiano uso" ("a remover of obstructions, and cures consumption, for the lamentable typhoid sufferers, daily use can cure them"; 111). This somewhat contradicts Mata's 1747 *Arte de Reposteria*, which claims that, among other things, chocolate can comfort the stomach and chest, yet at the same time also warns that it should not be used in excess or in impure forms, as it can also cause harm: "que no se ejecute muchas veces a causa de ser opilativo" ("it should not be employed too many times, as it can be obstructive"; 145). In spite of these differences of opinion, it does appear that many of the medical treatises do agree on chocolate as an appetite aid for those who previously were unenthusiastic about the prospect of eating, from Cortijo Herraiz to Vicente Lardizabal (1788), who asserts that there is no better appetite stimulant (15).

For the healthy, the use of chocolate is also controversial. Valverde starts the debate himself, outlining the reasons why chocolate could be considered both safe and dangerous in those who are already healthy. In his first conclusion on this matter, he states that it could be healthy, as long as certain conditions are met, such as the use of very simple ingredients and small quantities, particularly in cold weather: "En tiempo frío, por la mañana, y a lo más dos, o tres veces en la semana" ("In cold weather, in the morning, and at the maximum two or three times a week"; C2v). He outright proclaims that this contradicts the teachings of Barrios, who allows for three drinks a day. He then concludes it is in fact bad for the physically fit, as they do not follow his strict guidelines, and chocolate taken in larger amounts will, in his opinion, cause them harm (C3v).

Although there are those medical professionals who claim that chocolate is at best a cure-all and at worst harmless, there seems to be more of a consensus that overuse can be problematic on the one hand because the benefits can diminish over time, and on the other because a person who quits chocolate or decreases their intake may go through a sort of withdrawal. Valverde, before he even comes to his conclusions, reminds the reader that "aunque sea en si bueno el chocolate, se haga malo no sabiendo usar del" ("even if chocolate itself is good, it becomes bad through misuse"; C1), a sentiment that is reminiscent of the ninth stanza of the "Décima glosada," published almost exactly one century later: "No hay cosa mejor, si es bueno, / Ni cosa peor, si es malo" ("There is nothing better, if it is good, and nothing worse, if it is bad"; 119). In the endorsement notes to Cortijo Herraiz's book, one censor is much more explicit in his warnings of the dangers of overuse, recalling a cautionary tale he has heard: "Es verdad, que en mi tiempo se ha cantado, que de *tomar Chocolate murió una Reina; mas no tomara ella tanto, y no se mueriera*" ("It is true, in my time it has been said that from *drinking chocolate a Queen died; yet had she not drunk so much, she would not have died*"; n.p., emphasis in the original). The same censor concludes with a warning that no one should drink it at all, given that their ancestors and even they themselves had lived for years without it ever passing their lips, rather than risk the dangers of overuse. Lardizabal, writing some fifty years later, has the opposite concern regarding over-imbibing: that eventually the stomach becomes so familiar with the substance that its effects are dampened (20). In any case, the abuse of chocolate is universally condemned, even if the writers cannot agree on the reason.

From the time chocolate arrives full force in Spanish society in the late sixteenth century to the end of the eighteenth, and even beyond, the consensus on the medicinal benefits and/or drawbacks of its widespread use is about as clear as the drink itself. In spite of the ongoing debate in the medical community, however, we can trace an obvious trajectory of acceptance and praise in the literary sources: from Marradón's 1618 disparaging *Dialogue* as an early example of scepticism, to the brief mention of chocolate as a failed medicine in Quiñones de Benavente's 1657 *Entremés de la constreñida*; through Santos's 1663 *Día y noche de Madrid* – which places blame for illnesses not on the chocolate itself but rather on the method of preparation – to the beatification play of *Santa Rosa del Perú* (1671), analysed in the previous chapter, a play which answers not only the religious question on chocolate as a worthy tool of fasting but also addresses its medical use as a remedy for stomach pains, ending finally with the full acceptance of chocolate as a panacea in the "Décima glosada al chocolate" (first appearing in 1729 but reprinted and glossed throughout the eighteenth century, demonstrating widespread appeal of both the poem and chocolate). This chronological adoption of chocolate as healthy and medicinal in fiction does not follow the same path as the medical treatises; that course is far more meandering, as various physicians alternate between popular belief, the Church's teachings, and the experience of their patients. However, the more linear acceptance of chocolate in the literature may be more indicative of the social norms and a desire to legitimize this new-found habit.

Sinfully Delicious: The Darker Side of Chocolate

As we have seen, the debates on the validity of chocolate, from both the religious and medical points of view, were less than definitive in their conclusions. Although ultimately chocolate survives, and thrives, in Spanish society and beyond, it continues to be maligned for its potential dangers, which can be partially attributed to the discord among theological experts and physicians, but ultimately relates back to its origin in the New World. The religious debate concerns itself with the possible corrupting nature of the drink, but mainly through the lens of fasting, while the medical one focuses on health issues that arise from over-indulgence; this chapter will look beyond these relatively innocuous concerns and consider the more nefarious ones, including chocolate's role in inducing people to commit some of the deadly sins, its connections to witchcraft, and its inclusion as a trope in satirical or blasphemous works of literature.

The seven deadly sins as we know them today were first conceived in the fourth century and then shortly thereafter revised and codified into the Catholic canon by Pope Gregory I. Given the concerns out-lined in the medical and religious debates, it should not surprise us to find chocolate connected to three of the capital vices, namely greed, gluttony, and lust. Gluttony is possibly the most obvious of the three, given that it is the overindulgence in comestibles, echoing medical concerns of the day. Francisco de Quevedo, in his 1628 *Discurso de*

todos los diablos, Infierno enmendado, o El entremetido y la dueña,
personifies chocolate and tobacco as demons who have arrived in
Spain from the New World to avenge all the wrongs inflicted by the
conquistadors. In spite of calling them "el diablo del *Tabaco* y el diablo del *Chocolate*" ("the tobacco devil and the chocolate devil"; 49,
emphasis in original), he admits that they themselves are quite possibly not the true culprits: "que aunque yo los sospechaba, nunca los
tuve por diablos del todo" ("even though I suspected them, I never
really took them to be true devils"; 49). Instead, he places the blame
on the imbibers themselves: "siendo los chocolateros idólatras del
sorbo, que se eleven y le adoran, y se arroban" ("the chocoholics,
being idolaters of sipping, are the ones who place it on a pedestal,
adore it, and become entranced"; 49). Quevedo thus removes the culpability of overindulgence from the product and returns it to those
who drink to excess, turning them into idolaters who not only potentially hurt themselves but also break one of the Ten Commandments,
which would supersede their violation of the cardinal sins.

Notably, Quevedo begins with the caveat that his book is not meant
to call out anyone specifically or directly, and that only those looking
for offence – and perhaps feeling guilty already – will find it. Still,
Quevedo is known for his biting satire and thinly veiled slander, which
raises the question of whom he might be defaming with each devil
he describes. This is not the only time that he derides the actions of
the conquistadors and the consequences of the conquest on Spanish
society; his poem "Poderoso caballero" traces the life cycle of gold as
born in the Indies, dying in Spain, and being buried in Genoa, a satirical take on the mismanagement of riches by the Spanish monarchy.
In *Discurso de todos los diablos*, it would appear that Spain, and her
conquistadors, are on trial. The devils from the New World have come
to seek revenge, and, according to this passage, are doing a fine job
of it: "Éstos dijeron que ellos habían vengado a las Indias de España,
pues habían hecho más mal en meter acá los polvos y el humo y jícaras
y molinillos que el rey Católico a Colón y a Cortés y a Almagro y a

Pizarro; cuanto era mejor y más limpio y más glorioso ser muertos a mosquetazos y a lanzadas que a moquitas y estornudos y a regüeldos y a vaguidos y a tabardillos" ("They said that they had avenged the Indies in Spain, as these devils had done more damage in installing here the dust and smoke and cups and mills than the Catholic King had done to Columbus; to Cortés, Almagro and Pizarro; how much better and cleaner and more glorious was it to die of musket-shot and sword thrusts than from sniffles and sneezes, from belching, gases and putrefaction"; 49). Spain, under the thumb of these New World devils, has been reduced to weakness and illness. By including synecdochal references to tobacco ("los polvos y el humo") and chocolate ("jícaras y molinillos"), Quevedo demonstrates that these dangerous goods stand in for the Indigenous Other that aims to infiltrate the Spanish body and break it down from within, as opposed to the more glorious death on the battlefield. Ironically, we can devise from his own letters that he was a great fan of chocolate, albeit perhaps at a later date: "Asustado me tiene el sorbo de la mala nueva que corre de la pérdida de la flota, por el chocolate, cuando ya cojeaba una golosina discreta que teníamos; yo a intercesión de mi estómago lo dudo" ("The taste of the bad news of the loss of the fleet has me frightened, for the chocolate, as our modest supply of the sweet was already deficient; I, on behalf of my stomach, have my doubts"; Quevedo, qtd in Quevedo and Crosby 22).

Following the theme of gluttony, Ambrosio de Cuenca turns chocolate into an actual character in *A igual agravio, no hay duelo*, a *comedia* printed in 1660 in which the *gracioso* character is named Chocolate and is, as *graciosos* tend to be, characterized by his complaints of hunger, thirst, etc. from the start:

MELCHOR. Siempre tratas de comer.
CHOCOLATE. De barbas trata un barbero,

...

un doctor de los enfermos,

...

si veo que todos tratan
de su menester, yo quiero,
pues es lo que he menester,
tratar de comer hambriento ... (470–1)[1]

MELCHOR. You're always trying to eat.

CHOCOLATE. A barber handles beards ... a doctor, his patients ... if I see
that all others address their needs, then I want, as it is what I need, to
try to eat when hungry ...

By comparing himself to a barber who takes care of beards and a
doctor who treats patients, Chocolate converts eating into his profession, something that he must tend to out of obligation and to gain his
livelihood. Without his hunger to define him, he is not himself. He is
gluttony personified.

Beyond the normal tendencies towards base desires, *graciosos* with
the name Chocolate can also play into the double meaning of their
name to refer to both self and the drink. In *A igual agravio*, Cuenca's
gracioso offers himself up if there is no other food to go around:

CHOCOLATE. Si quieres hacer gran fiesta
dame en jícaras metido,
yo sé que habrá quien me beba,
porque beben de ladrillo
polvo en mi nombre, y no hay tienda
donde de maíz, y habas,
no hagan conmigo cajetas,
muy vestido de achiote,
de pimientos, y canela,
el verano estoy nevado,
y tal vez puesto en sorbeta,
y el invierno muy caliente:
no me perdonan las dueñas,

no hay ya lacayo en el mundo,

que la sangre no me beba:

por de Guajaca me venden,

y es imposible en tal Era,

que aún no soy de Guayaquil.

MELCHOR. Siempre has de hablar frioleras. (475)

CHOCOLATE. If you want to have a great party, serve me in *jícaras*, I know that someone will drink me, since they drink from bricks of powder in my name, and there isn't a shop were they don't make sweets out of me with corn and beans, all dressed up in achiote, pepper, and cinnamon; in summer I'm snowy and may be found in sherbet, in winter, warm: the ladies refuse to give me up, there isn't a footman on earth that won't drink my blood: they label me "Oaxaca" for sale, even though it's impossible, as I am not even from Guayaquil.

MELCHOR. You're always talking in riddles.

All of this *gracioso*'s wordplay centres on the quality and quantity of the chocolate to be drunk, and his own ever-present hunger. The bricks of powder reference the way chocolate is manufactured in order to be shipped to Spain, while the addition of corn and beans to the drink alludes to the Indigenous methods of preparation, and achiote, pepper, and cinnamon are all spices used on both sides of the Atlantic to enhance flavour and appearance. Finally, naming Oaxaca and Guayaquil, two of the major agricultural centres for chocolate production, is another reference to quality, as chocolate from Oaxaca was considered to be the superior product, while that of Guayaquil was seen as inferior, often thought of as the "cacao of the poor" (Coe and Coe 185). Thus, in spite of being sold as a superior chocolate from Oaxaca, Chocolate is telling his audience that he is not even of the poorer quality. Still, it seems that he has no lack of imbibers.

Calderón's Chocolate is less interested in sustenance, but still plays on his name's dual nature:

VIOLANTE. Chocolate, cómo así
    entras? No ves ...
CHOCOLATE. No te espante
    que por la mañana puede
    entrar cualquier Chocolate
    a visitar una dama.
VIOLANTE. ¿A qué vienes aquí?
CHOCOLATE. A darte
    un recado de mi amo,
    y a saber de ti. (*Gustos y disgustos* 14)

VIOLANTE. Chocolate, how did you get in here? Don't you see ...
CHOCOLATE. Don't be afraid, in the morning any Chocolate can get in to
    visit a lady.
VIOLANTE. Why are you here?
CHOCOLATE. To give you a note from my master and find out about you.

Chocolate, as a man, is not supposed to be in a lady's private room, but as a servant, his presence is less likely to cause scandal. By using his name, he emphasizes the double meaning: both chocolate the drink and Chocolate, her suitor's servant, have easy access to a lady's chambers. Although not explicit, this Chocolate's self-referentiality is also sexualized. He has entered into the bedroom of a woman of a higher class, who reminds him that he should not be there, and when he responds, he tells her that it is the most normal thing in the world for there to be chocolate in a lady's room, while also using his own name to indicate that it is not that unusual to find the servant of a suitor there either. This is reinforced by the *recado* sent by his master to Violante, which can be translated either as "note" or "gift of affection." Thus, the Chocolate sent to Violante is a reminder of their promise to each other, since Violante and Vicente, Chocolate's master, have already married in secret and are living as husband and wife. The real danger that Chocolate's presence in her room presents is the possibility that he will be found by someone not aware of Violante's legal status as a married woman, who would assume that she had allowed Vicente into her room. As a presumed unmarried woman, her honour would be damaged, possibly beyond repair. Calderón's naming of the *gracioso* here moves chocolate's sinful nature away from greed and gluttony and into the realm of lust.

Chocolate's connection to sexuality is one that persists, with the oft-repeated theory that some women prefer the edible over the act, and the association was present even as chocolate was first introduced to European society. Aside from Díaz del Castillo's initial observation of Montezuma's "access" to women, facilitated through chocolate, we also find in Francisco Hernández de Toledo's *Historia de las plantas de Nueva España* (written after his trip between 1571 and 1576 to Mexico) reference to the aphrodisiacal nature of the drink: "La propiedad de la bebida compuesta es excitar el apetito venéreo" ("The attributes of this mixed drink excite the sexual appetite"; 913). Similarly, in a poem to an unnamed lady, Antonio Hurtado de Mendoza (1690)[2] compares chocolate to love, listing its contradictory elements and effects in such a way that the reader is left unsure whether it is chocolate or love that hurts so much:

> ¿qué dé gusto y no mate?,
> cosas tiene de amor el chocolate.
> ¿Qué ha de estar abrasando en punto ardiente
> para tener sazón?, ¿qué dulcemente
> ha de picar?, ¿qué ha de abrasar el pecho
> dejando el apetito satisfecho?
> ¿Qué sustente? ¿Qué sueño no consienta?
> ¿Qué engañe con azúcar su pimienta?
> ¿Qué haya su molinillo, y que la jícara
> pueda más agradar cuanto más pícara?
> ¿Qué haya su poco de agua y su puchero?
> Basta que es por la fe de caballero

(mala rabia le mate)
definición de amor el chocolate. (Hurtado de Mendoza 3:209)

What gives pleasure and doesn't kill? Chocolate has some of love's characteristics. Must it be burning to a boiling point to have flavour? What stings so sweetly? What hugs the chest leaving a satisfied appetite? What sustains? What indulges dreams? What tricks with sugar its pepper? What's in its mill and cup that pleases more the more it stings? What has so little water and a pot? It is enough, by a gentleman's faith (may bad rage kill him), that the definition of love is chocolate. (Trans. RG & EC)

As Olympia B. González demonstrates, Hurtado de Mendoza was no stranger to the intimate lives of Madrid's courtesans, and his poems often reflect two subjects that profoundly occupied their daily lives: "la comida, como elemento de la vida social, y la relación amorosa carnal" ("food, as an element of their social lives, and their sexual relationships"; 237). Thus, chocolate becomes a stand-in for love, and the narrator uses the combination of sweet and spicy ingredients to remind the reader that often we want what hurts us most: "¿Qué ha de estar abrasando en punto ardiente / para tener sazón?" ("Must it be burning to a boiling point to have flavour?") and "¿qué ha de abrasar el pecho / dejando el apetito satisfecho?" ("What hugs the chest leaving a satisfied appetite?") allude to the potentially damaging nature of an illicit love affair as much as they do to the flavours of chocolate: the imbiber of both pushes the limits to enjoy their indulgence more fully. "¿Qué engañe con azúcar su pimienta?" ("What tricks with sugar its pepper?") asks if sweetness really can cover up the bite of pepper in chocolate; or, if the fleeting pleasure of love will be enough to ignore the potentially disastrous consequences of dishonour. In spite of the clear warning that love, like chocolate, is only best when it is most dangerous, the narrator surrenders himself to it in the end.

Perhaps not surprisingly, given its sexual connotations as well as its origins in the New World, chocolate is tied more closely with women and, therefore, with the potential for witchcraft. The New World was seen as the territory of the devil; with no previous contact with Christianity, the rituals and ceremonies of the Indigenous peoples were seen as demonic, as was their polytheism. In the early *Du chocolat: Dialogue entre un medecin, un indien & un bourgeois*, Marradón uses an Indigenous character to denounce the New World, its inhabitants, and its potential exports: "Je vous supplie dites-moi si le *Chocolate* est aussi méchant & aussi mal sain que le *Tabac*?" ("I beg you to tell me if chocolate is just as evil and unhealthy as tobacco?"; 172–3; trans. Pupillo). Although it takes him some time to respond, since he first discusses chocolate's different uses and its similarities to almond milk, the doctor eventually concedes that excessive use of chocolate should be criticized in the same way as tobacco's (180). Still, the Indigenous character persists in his badmouthing of his own people and their influence on Spaniards, particularly the women: "Où comme les Dames ont usé de ce breuvage il leur a donné occasion de se venger de leurs jalousies, en apprenant & se servante des sortilèges des Indiennes qui en sont grandes maitresses, comme estant enseignées par le Diable, c'est pourquoi les personnes sages doivent éviter la fréquentation des Indiennes pour le seul soupçon de sortilège" ("Now that Women have become accustomed to this beverage it gives them the occasion to avenge their jealousies, learning and using the curses of the Indian women, who are great masters [of witchcraft]; it is like being taught by the Devil himself. This is why wise persons should avoid mingling with Indians due to the mere suspicion of evil spells"; 186–7; trans. Pupillo).[3] Thus Marradón places the authority on what is and is not dangerous in the New World into the hands of one of their own, who ultimately betrays his homeland. If the Indian of the dialogue believes that contact with other Indigenous peoples could bring misfortune, why would a Spaniard take the risk? The New World was seen as the realm of the devil, a remnant of a world divided between duelling deities, so a comestible that comes from such a place must have some residual evil lurking inside.

The interlude *La boda de Juan Rana* (attributed to Francisco de Avellaneda in 1664 and Gerónimo de Cáncer in 1691)[4] picks up on the connection between jealousy and chocolate:

MÚSICOS. Parece el *chocolate*
   mucho a los celos,
   pues al que más le sabe, sabe
   que quita el sueño. (32)

  MUSICIANS. It seems that chocolate resembles jealousy quite a bit, given
   that he who tastes it most knows it steals sleep.

In this case, however, rather than a person using the beverage to get revenge and inflict pain on another, it is chocolate itself that takes its revenge on the over-imbiber, enough to keep him from sleeping, just as jealousy does.

In spite of the warnings, particularly from Marradón's Indian, that Indigenous peoples and the goods found in the New World are in league with (or perhaps even are themselves) devils, chocolate still makes its way across the Atlantic and into Spanish society. Calderón de la Barca alludes to the dark connection to magic in his interlude *La garapiña* (1678), a *mojiganga* that consists of a suitor who attempts to find a cure for his prospective love's woes. He brings her a strange concoction, in which chocolate is mixed with a variety of other drinks, a mixture that invites disgust and rejection on her part. Still, he spurs her on, reminding her that all of the ingredients are ones that normally would be well known and acceptable on their own, and their mixture together in one particular vessel should not surprise or concern her:

BLASA ¡En redoma!
GALÁN ¿Qué te espanta?
   Que si estas son las bebidas
   familiares de las damas,
   ¿qué mucho, si familiares
   son, que en redoma las traiga? (lines 249–53)

BLASA. In a jug!

GALAN. What frightens you so? If these are the familiar drinks of women, how much of a surprise, if indeed they are familiar, is it that they must be brought in jugs? (Trans. RG & EC)

Evangelina Rodríguez and Antonio Tordera, in their online edition of the interlude, note that "familiar" can have the meaning of knowing or being acquainted with someone or something, but it also had by the seventeenth century the more sinister connotation of an object that allowed for communication with the devil; they make note of another instance in Vélez de Guevara's *Diablo cojuelo*, in which a demon is trapped in a "redoma" (253n). If such drinks are "familiars" to women in Calderón's world, then chocolate's use can be seen as a conduit for spells.

In Quiñones de Benavente's *Entremés cantado de el mago*, the women all sing about their nonsensical habits and eventually proclaim themselves devils. One in particular, Rufina, claims that "Yo, sabiéndome mal, tomo / por vanidad chocolate" ("I, knowing myself to be unwell, drink chocolate in vain"), to which the chorus replies with their constant refrain, "Locura bien grande" ("That's quite the insanity"; lines 114–16). Of course, "sabiéndome mal" could also be translated as "tasting bad," which would play on the double meaning of "saber" in Spanish and make the connection back to chocolate. Although in *El mago* the women's proclamations of demonic affiliation and the use of chocolate as a cure are not directly connected, there are many other cases in which chocolate and magic are linked. Perhaps the most prominent example of this is in Ana Caro Mallén de Soto's *Valor, agravio y mujer* (1651):

TOMILLO. Despúes que bebí de aquel
    negro chocolate, o mixto
    de varias cosas que Flora
    me brindó, estoy aturdido,

los ojos no puedo abrir.
Sale Flora.
FLORA. Siguiendo vengo a Tomillo
Por si ha obrado el chocolate.
TOMILLO. Doy al diablo lo que miro
si lo veo; aquí me acuesto
un rato. ¡Qué bien mullido
está el suelo!
Échase.
No parece
sino que aposta se hizo
para quebrarme los huesos.
Esto es hecho. No he podido
sustentar la competencia;
sueño, a tus fuerzas me rindo.
Duerme. (3.3263–79)

TOMILLO. Ever since I drank from that black chocolate, or mixture of various things that Flora offered me, I am bewildered, I can barely open my eyes. *Flora enters.*
FLORA. I'm following Tomillo to see if the chocolate has worked its magic.
TOMILLO. I'll give the devil his due, if what I see is what I think it is; but here I'll rest a while. How soft is this floor! *Lies down.* It seems that it was made just for relaxing my bones. That's it. I can't compete; dreams, I give myself over to you. *Falls asleep.*

Flora has apparently given Tomillo a drink that makes him fall asleep, although Tomillo's drowsy exposition is the only on-stage reference to chocolate in the play. Flora was certainly aware of the effect her concoction would have on Tomillo as she follows him on stage to make sure it is working and, once he is subdued, proceeds to rifle through his pockets in search of his coin purse. Overall, Flora's employment of chocolate to overpower her victim is innocuous in comparison to other applications, but it is still an excellent illustration of the use of chocolate in casting spells or administering substances undetected.

In the *Entremés del nigromántico*, we find a young man, Lorenzo, who has stumbled upon the lair of a necromancer, who seems to be able to control Lorenzo with just his voice. Even though his first reaction is of horror, he seems unable to leave, and allows the sorcerer to remove his boots, almost force-feed him food and chocolate, and shave his beard (*El nigromántico* 24–5). Finally, the necromancer gives him some magical glasses that allow him to spy on his wife, who has recently kicked him out of their home. It is thus that he is able to see her making preparations for her lover, the sacristan Chispilla, to arrive in his absence. He thanks the wizard for his help in opening his eyes to the truth and prepares to kill his wife, to which the necromancer replies that it has all been a joke. Although the chocolate itself is not used to enchant or trick Lorenzo, its presence in the necromancer's home and its reception by Lorenzo do make the connection not only with hospitality, as Amado Doblas claims ("En el V centenario II" 341), but also with black magic.

To underline the ability of chocolate to mask other elements, in her introduction to the first published version of a seventeenth-century, anonymous, and satirical Sephardic manuscript on chocolate and the Inquisition, *Relación verdadera del gran sermón*, Mabel González Quiroz explains that chocolate was a popular vessel for other, less appetizing ingredients in witches' potions: "Por su sabor amargo y la variedad de especias que podía contener, el chocolate era el medio perfecto para disfrazar los sabores de ciertos ingredientes obligatorios de dichas pócimas, a todas luces repulsivos, pues no pocas veces contenían, por ejemplo, restos de corazón de cuervo, excremento, carne humana y sangre menstrual" ("Because of its bitter taste and the variety of spices it could contain, chocolate was the perfect medium to disguise the flavours of other necessary ingredients in said potions, all of which were utterly repulsive, as they more often than not contained such things as the remains of a crow's heart, excrement, human flesh, and menstrual blood"; 29), all of which point to nefarious acts, given their revolting nature.[5] Although this might seem exaggerated to the modern reader, we find a similar notice, dated 28 February 1657, in the *Avisos de Don Jerónimo de Barrionuevo*, a compendium of reports sent from the court to the decan of Zaragoza, that states "Predicó en San Gil al Consejo Real un fraile descalzo y dijo había llegado a sus pies un penitente que mezclaba el chocolate con tierra de difuntos, que lo engrasaba mucho y hacía muy bueno, y que con esto lo vendía a subido precio, Es cierto" ("In San Gil there is a barefooted priest who preached to the Royal Council; he told of a penitent who came crawling to him, speaking of a chocolate that he mixed with the earth of the dead, which made it quite fatty and very nice, and as such he could sell it at an elevated price. This is true"; Barrionuevo 64). How Barrionuevo knew that it was a truthful notice we cannot be sure, but it was clearly considered a possibility, as Calderón refers to the same special ingredient in his entremés *Las lenguas* (1670–7):[6]

> NEGRO. Si viene buscando neglo,
>   que molamo chocolate,
>   aquí za turo aderezo
>   harina de maíz, billota,
>   almendra, almilion tenemo,
>   y pala que haga glaza,
>   le echamo tierra de muelto;
>   espelate, que ya salgo. (*Entremés famoso de las lenguas* 6)

> NEGRO. If you come looking for negros who grind chocolate, here we have all kinds of dressing, corn flour, acorn, almond, we have them by the lot, and to make it extra fatty, we add some earth of the dead; wait, I'm coming out now. (Trans. RG & EC)

It is not, in fact, a reference made simply to provoke disgust or dark humour in the audience; rather, earth taken from graveyards has long been considered to hold magical properties and is used to curse or hurt the person who ingests it, giving this passage a darker interpretation than its ridiculing tone implies.

Returning to the *Gran sermón*, González Quiroz claims that, in spite of the malevolent connotations attributed to it, chocolate also gained a reputation for its aphrodisiacal qualities, which put it into direct conflict with the Church and Inquisition (29). In this same "great sermon" – which consists of a series of stories that ostensibly celebrate the virtues of chocolate – we find the story of a Japanese king who, given chocolate to treat his pains, is not only instantaneously cured but also, feeling rather amorous after breaking his three-day fast, is sure that he can "enamore con ellas / a viudas, a casadas, o, a doncellas" ("win over all of them: widows, married women, even virgins"; 203). This miraculous cure is even more amazing when we consider that the pharmacist was so concerned about the potion he was instructed to create that he took steps to distance himself from the possibly disastrous results:

Mandose esta receta al boticario,
y él la hizo copiar por un notario,
temiendo era veneno,
porque no la halló escrita en su Galeno,
y protestó de hacerla puntualmente
delante mucha gente,
porque si el Rey muriera,
de la culpa la ley lo eximiera. (202)

The prescription was sent to the pharmacist, who in turn had it copied by a notary, fearing that it was poisonous, as he could not find it written down by Galen, and he protested greatly in front of many people, so that if the king were to die, he would be exonerated of any legal guilt.

The pharmacist's precaution underlines how minor the distinction is between chocolate as a magical, healing concoction and a dangerous, poisonous potion. It also shows the distrust associated with a New World good: if it is not mentioned by Galen, it is either unknown to one of the greatest ancient doctors or simply considered unworthy of his attentions. Either way, it is suspect as a legitimate medicine.[7]

As González Quiroz points out, the negative and witchcraft associations are derived directly from chocolate's New World origin: "A menudo, el chocolate estuvo asociado a la brujería, actividad por lo general ejercida por mujeres que, en el caso de América, solían ser de raza negra, aborigen, mestizas o mulatas. Uno de los motivos más comunes para recurrir a los servicios de estas mujeres eran las consultas de tipo amoroso" ("Often, chocolate was associated with witchcraft, an activity generally undertaken by women, who, in the case of the Americas, tended to be African, Aboriginal, or a mixture thereof. One of the most common motives for resorting to the services of such women was to resolve questions of love"; 28).[8] Interestingly, the *Gran sermón* which González Quiroz is prefacing with these remarks is set outside of both Europe and the Americas, with the vast majority of the miracles being performed in Asia and Africa, mainly by travelling Iberians who share the magical properties of chocolate with their hosts. In fact, there is only one reference to the American origins of the bean, in a sung prayer included in the preamble to the manuscript. Thus, in spite of the prejudices against connections to New World sorcery, it is Spaniards themselves who are portrayed by the anonymous author as the disseminators of this potentially black magic. The author's presumed identity as a Sephardic Jew[9] – not to mention the material itself – would be enough to make us consider the work satirical; thus the erasure of the Indigenous associations and the emphasis on Spanish propagation contribute to the blasphemous nature of the text, and of chocolate itself. Where previously missions – including the expeditions to the New World – to spread Spanish superiority would focus on the promulgation of the Catholic religion, here we find chocolate as the miraculous cure-all and most significant feature of contact with Iberian travellers, replacing the missionary's purpose of spreading religion with the spread of chocolate throughout the non-Christian world. It is thus that the *Gran sermón* removes any culpability on the part of the Indigenous peoples of the Americas and places it squarely on Spaniards who have overindulged and given a ridiculous amount of importance to chocolate in their daily lives. This is the true subversive nature of the *Gran sermón*. Early literary sources place chocolate in the realm of the New World, usually being provided to Spaniards by Indigenous peoples or, at most, by the *indianos* – those men who set out to win their fortunes in the Indies and who have since returned to Spain – while later sources attribute the sale and preparation of the drink primarily to *negros*. Both versions allow for any evil or magical properties to be attributable to the Other. The *Gran sermón*, on the other hand, places the Other on the receiving end of chocolate, codifying Spaniards as the providers of chocolate and all its potential connections with religion, medicine, and even the dark arts, for better or worse.

This critique of Spanish society comes at the same time that the last Hapsburg ruler was known for his gluttonous fondness for chocolate. Carlos II, known as "el hechizado" ("the Cursed"), was purported to have been poisoned by his own mother, using chocolate to hide the taste of a dead man's brain, which had been dissolved therein to render Carlos ineffectual as both a leader and progenitor of the next royal generation (Maura, *Supersticiones* 234–5).[10] His predilection for chocolate was so well known that in a letter to the Queen, his guardian and regent, an anonymous *arbitrista*[11] notes that among the greatest expenses of the court that need to be curbed are "las galas, la ostentación, el lucimiento, el chocolate y el coche" ("the galas, ostentation, showiness, chocolate, and coach"; qtd by Maura, *Carlos II* 482). Of the list, "ostentation" and "showiness" are more vague qualities, whereas the galas, chocolate, and coach are concrete items that could easily be quantified and therefore reduced. The quantifiable goods are of particular interest, as we must suspect that in order for these individual items to be singled out, there must have been public knowledge of the court's – and in particular this King's – overindulgence in such things.

In the fourth episode of the *Gran sermón*, a priest, upon hearing of an incurably possessed man, decides to attempt an exorcism via chocolate. The man, the leader or "Cam" of Tartary – a region inhabited by Turks and Mongols from the late medieval period up into the twentieth century – is protected from the priest by his secretary, who notes that any convert to Christianity will be martyred. The secretary also delivers a scathing diatribe against the imperial nature of Spain and the Inquisition:

> tu reino está perdido,
> por querer salvar almas con violencia,
> y es contra la divina omnipotencia
> como ya tengo dicho;
> y así por la virtud desse capricho,
> (de todo buen juicio, abominado)
> sabemos que aquel reino es despoblado,
> y por andar allá con tales leyes,
> la España es vituperio de los reyes,
> porque no es fe divina,
> la fe que causa al reino su ruina,
> sino embuste inventado,
> para vivir en miserable estado;
> y a su Inquisición yo la imagino,
> un puro Don Quijote a lo divino
> porque es gran bobería acreditada
> fundar divinidad en lo que es nada. (131; IV.90–106)

... your kingdom is lost, because it wishes to save souls with violence, against all divine omnipotence, as I have already said; and thus, by virtue of such a whim (abhorred by all good judgment), we know that that kingdom is sparsely populated, and for following such laws, Spain is the disgrace of its kings, because it cannot be a divine faith that brings ruin to its kingdom, but rather a fabrication, to make you live in such a miserable state; and I can only imagine that your Inquisition is a purely divine Don Quixote, as it is greatly renowned idiocy to base divinity on nothingness.[12]

This scathing attack on the Spanish Empire is reminiscent of the critiques by Bartolomé de las Casas, the Spanish priest in the New World who warned that treating the Indigenous peoples as slaves and forcing them violently into the Catholic Church would only cause more problems and violence. Still, the secretary relents and allows for the chocolate to be administered, but only by himself, without the help of the priest, who, despite the admonishments of the secretary, still hopes to take advantage of the opportunity to perform baptism at the same time. The possible religious element having been removed, the chocolate is administered, and, much to the surprise of the priest, the Cam is cured instantaneously (137–9). The *Gran sermón* is able to ridicule church and empire at the same time, while also exposing the ridiculous ideology of chocolate as a cure-all or miracle worker, as well as proving that chocolate, like medicine in general, does not need Catholicism or blessings in order to function, since it was never truly a Christian good.

Not all of the allusions to the magic powers of chocolate are negative in their undertones, but there is an otherworldliness to a substance that can accomplish anything from knocking a man out to reviving his libido. Where chocolate is presented as a cure, it is often seen as a miracle, and yet in many ways a sacrilegious one: Captain Castro de Torres's *Panegírico al chocolate* (1640) gives the reader the impression that chocolate not only is the perfect drink but also can do no wrong, even attributing it with suicide prevention: "Que no hay hombre en el mundo que se mate, / Si una vez ha bebido chocolate" ("There isn't a man in the world who would kill himself, if even once he has drunk chocolate"; 13). Not only this, but Torres bills the drink as a life-saving elixir that can also serve as a fountain of youth, and places it above gold and silver in value, echoing Indigenous valuations. Although Torres does not discuss it in comparison with Christian values, Antonio Hurtado de Mendoza leaves no doubt: "sin duda el chocolate no es cristiano" ("Without a doubt, chocolate is not Christian"; Hurtado de Mendoza 3:210). If this is so, then praising it as miraculous would actually be blasphemous.

Along with the satire provided in the *Gran sermón*, and, of course, that of Quevedo, Hurtado de Mendoza provides us with three exemplary poems that satirize the intense hold chocolate has achieved over the peninsula in such a short period. His poems equate chocolate with love and play on words to reinforce the ludicrous popularity of the drink:

Aunque a picarte no llega
hermosísima Señora,
ningún chocolate ahora,
que se toma, o que se juega,
ya que amor también te niega
su picazón, toma aquí
el naipe, entretente, y di
que de un alma que ha ganado
lo perdido, y lo pecado
todo queda para mí. (Hurtado de Mendoza 2:87)

Although no chocolate comes now to excite you, beautiful Señora, to drink, or to play with, since love also denies you its prick, take the cards here, amuse yourself, and say that, of a soul that has won what was lost, all the sins are left for me.

By using the verb "picar" and its derived noun "picazón," Hurtado de Mendoza opens up the interpretation of chocolate in this poem to be anything from "exciting" to "bothersome" to the beautiful Señora, who has been deprived of both chocolate and love, and thus of amusement in her life. I chose to translate these words as "excite" and "prick" respectively because I interpret Hurtado de Mendoza's poem to be a critique of the lavish lifestyle that is embodied by Spanish women who overindulge in both chocolate and lovers. Given Hurtado de Mendoza's close connection to the court, and his known penchant for satirizing the love lives of the nobility, as well as for mixing metaphors of lovemaking and food, this interpretation holds true.[13]

Although María de Zayas was also well known for her critique of the many hazards that faced women in early modern Spain, she is surprisingly quiet on the topic of chocolate. Her first compilation, *Novelas amorosas y ejemplares*, first published in 1637, makes no mention of the drink at all, while her second collection, *Desengaños amorosos* (1647), refers to it only once, in the introduction that sets up the frame story for her interwoven tales of women's woes. Setting the scene, she mentions the decoration, attending musicians, and, of course, the feast that is laid out for the guests: "sin que faltase el amigo chocolate que en todo se halla, como la mala ventura" ("dear chocolate, which is found everywhere, just like misfortune, does not fail to appear"; 120). Since it is not a feature of the first book, its inclusion in her second tome perhaps indicates the rapid popularization of the drink between the 1630s and 1640s. Still, Lope de Vega's *La Dorotea* (1632) makes brief mention of it, in spite of having an *indiano* protagonist and abundant mention of the New World and its fruits, and even then, it is only to have a Spanish woman reject the offer of that gift in favour of a silver cup:

BELA. Laurencio.

LAURENCIO. Señor.

BELA. Dale a Gerarda aquella tembladera de plata para que haga chocolate, y una de las dos cajas.

LAURENCIO. (¡Qué presto dejarán en cueros a mi amo estas bellacas! ¿Mas que volvemos a las Indias en calzas y en jubón como el Hijo Pródigo?) Tome, madre.

GERARDA. La tembladera tomo; las cajas guarda, que el chocolate que yo bebo, por acá se hace en San Martín y en Coca. (80–1)

BELA. Laurencio.

LAURENCIO. Yes, sir.

BELA. Give Gerarda that silver cup to make chocolate with, and one of the two boxes.

LAURENCIO. (How quickly will these unscrupulous women leave my master in little more than his skin! Are we to go back to the Indies in breeches and undershirts, like the Prodigal Son?) Here you are, mother.

GERARDA. I'll take the silver cup; you can keep your boxes, the chocolate that I drink from around here is made in San Martín and in Coca.

Donald McGrady, in his notes on the Real Academia Española edition of this play, tells us that the "chocolate" that Gerarda refers to as being made near to Madrid is actually wine (81n); she has no interest in or desire for the New World drink, but is following the pattern of many of the *indiano* plays, which show Spanish women to be happily inclined towards separating the *indiano* from his new-found wealth.

Returning to the Zayas quote, we find that she not only demonstrates that chocolate is found everywhere you turn by the publication of her second anthology but also equates it with "la mala ventura." Women in Zayas's worldview are always already ill-fated, particularly if they are also beautiful, and that bad luck is as abundant as chocolate, apparently.[14] Still, this is far from the direct critiques of chocolate as a familiar for witches, or a temptation to sin, demonstrating that it was not one of the greater evils facing her fellow woman, at least not for Zayas, for whom men are women's greatest adversaries.[15]

Continuing his commentary on the corruption of Spanish women by the New World influence, Hurtado de Mendoza writes another *décima*, this time incriminating the *indiano* for his lies and manipulations, including the use of chocolate to gain access to noble women:

> Si os pica el vivo acicate
> de este indiano, gentilhombre
> será (mentido su nombre)
> milagro, y no chocolate.
> El que dulcemente os bate
> la espuela, diestro y galán
> con qué maña o ademán
> anima este desaliento,
> en figura de pimiento
> no le conozca Galbán. (Hurtado de Mendoza 3:208)

> If the lively spur of this *indiano* pricks you, he'll be a gentleman (his name, a lie), and it will be a miracle, and not chocolate. He who sweetly churns the spurs, skilled and gallantly with such ability and movement, will encourage this despondency, disguised as a pepper; not even Galbán will recognize him.[16]

Hurtado de Mendoza again employs the verb "picar" to insinuate a relationship between a woman and, in this case, an *indiano* who might use chocolate in his attempts to woo her, but he will need a miracle to win her over and fool everyone else into believing he is something that he is not, a gentleman in name, which is to say, from a family of noble background.

In the play *El mayorazgo figura* by Alonso Castillo Solórzano (1640), chocolate is presented as symbolic of the New World and the riches available there. Marino, the *gracioso*, pretending to be a suitor who has just returned from the Indies, inquires about the status of chocolate in Spain:

MARINO. ¿Engullís bien chocolate?
ELENA. En Madrid se ha introducido

tanto que todos le toman,
hombres, mujeres y niños.
MARINO. Hacen bien los madrileños.
Yo traigo en catorce líos
cosa de ochocientas cajas. (2.1368–74)

MARINO. Do you guzzle down chocolate?
ELENA. In Madrid, it has been so well introduced that everyone drinks it,
men, women, and children.
MARINO. The *madrileños* do well for themselves. In fourteen lots I bring
some eight hundred boxes.

Notably, the verb Marino uses to ask Elena about her consumption
is not "beber" or "tomar," which would be translated as "to drink,"
or even "sorber" ("to sip/slurp"), which would echo Quevedo's sentiment both in fiction and correspondence, but rather "enguillir," "to
guzzle/gobble down," which evokes a much more visceral scene. The
act of guzzling or gobbling something seems much more gluttonous
than sipping or drinking, and suggests much more fervent, coarse
activity. This vulgarity foreshadows Elena's true character, which is
exactly why Marino is faking his status as a rich *indiano*: to find out
for Elena's real suitor whether her intentions are true or if she is much
more materialistic than she portrays herself. As soon as the fake *indiano* has elaborated his goods and inheritance, however, she reveals her
self-serving interests, stating "A él me inclino" ("I am inclined towards
him"; 2.1383). It is an oft-repeated trope in early modern dramas
that the *indiano*, newly rich and unversed in the ways of upper-class
society, is easily duped by women of the lower nobility looking to
use him for his money and discard him for a suitor of more suitable
status once his coffers run dry. The mention of chocolate, along with
other recognizable New World goods, connects Elena directly to this
trope and growing concerns of greed associated with the return of the
indianos. The true *indiano* of *El mayorazgo fingido*, Don Diego, is at

least savvy enough to test his potential bride-to-be and saves himself from being completely defrauded. In spite of the potential financial dangers for the man who returns newly rich to Spanish society, there were equal risks to staying in Spain in the first place, as a popular refrain of the time explains: "Él que va a las Indias es loco, y él que no va es bobo" ("He who goes to the Indies is crazy, and he who does not is foolish"; Correas 94). It would appear that the Spanish man of the lower nobility who wishes to climb the social ladder is stuck between a rock and a hard place: either go to the Indies, risking his life, hoping to come back rich, only to be taken advantage of by conniving women and their rapacious families; or stay home, but have little chance for upward social mobility or prospects for marriage.

Chocolate thus becomes a marker of knowledge of the New World, something that the *indiano* can use to prove himself as someone who has gained everything that he might need from his transatlantic trip, both financially and socially. In Tirso de Molina's *La villana de Vallecas* (1627), the *indiano* Don Pedro loses everything he has brought with him to show his wealth and worth to his potential wife. When he finally arrives in Madrid to meet her and her family, he finds that the man who stole his luggage has usurped his position as Serafina's suitor. Pedro's servant, Agudo, demands that the man's knowledge be tested, as he is sure that the Pedro-imposter has never set foot in Mexico:

... respóndame a este argumento:
las islas de Barlovento
¿cuántas son? ¿Dónde es Campeche?
¿Cómo se coge el cacao?
Guarapo, ¿qué es entre esclavos?
¿Qué fruta dan los guayabos? (2.2079–84)[17]

I demand that he responds to this line of questioning: the Barlovento islands: how many are there? Where is Campeche? How do they pick cacao beans? *Guarapo*, what does it mean among the slaves? What fruit does the guava tree give?

Agudo's questions indicate that only someone who had spent significant time in the Indies would be expected to know the answers,
and the inclusion of the cacao bean demonstrates that the process
by which chocolate came into being was still very much New World
knowledge. Unfortunately for the real Don Pedro, Serafina and her
family refuse to test the impersonator, as he has already showered
them with the gifts Don Pedro intended to give them, in corroboration of his status as a wealthy *indiano*. For their trouble, Don Pedro
and Agudo are declared madmen by Serafina and ordered out of her
house.

Interestingly, the lack of comprehension on the part of Serafina
and her father, Don Gómez, elevates Don Pedro as superior to non-
indiano Spaniards, at least in his own understanding of the world:

> Agudo, ¿aquésta es España?
>
> ...
>
> Los que de España pasaban,
> nos decían en mi tierra
> que los dobleces y engaños
> eran naturales de ella;
> bien lo experimento en mí,
> pues en Madrid entro apenas,
> cuando confunden mi dicha
> los laberintos de Creta.
> No hallo nobleza sencilla,
> amistad que permanezca;
> caballos de Troya son
> cuantos la corte sustenta. (2.2293–2307)

> Agudo, is this Spain? ... Those who came from Spain told us that double-
> crosses and tricks were second nature there; now I'm experiencing it for
> myself, barely arrived in Madrid and the labyrinths of Crete have entan-
> gled my good luck. I find no unassuming nobility, or lasting friendship;
> the court maintains only Trojan horses.

As someone who appears to have spent most of his life in Mexico, Don Pedro is unaccustomed to the treacheries of Madrid's courtly intrigue and finds Spanish society quite contemptible. Unfortunately, lacking proof of his origins and finding himself shunned by his prospective wife, he is an outsider without means to break the barriers of the society he desires to enter yet scorns at the same time. That Serafina would reject her genuine suitor, who proves himself in word and deed to be superior, for the fraud, simply because he showers her with gifts, demonstrates once again that the driving force of the Spanish nobility was greed. Once their true identities are revealed, Serafina immediately announces her love for the true Don Pedro, who is set to inherit far more than what was originally stolen from him, and all is forgiven, proving once again the ingenuous nature of the *indiano* – and the avaricious nature of young Spanish women.

Although the medical and religious debates were far more formalized, both were eventually discredited or, at the very least, ignored by the vast majority of the lay population. Two almost simultaneous edicts in April 1681 – one by the Apostolic Nuncio and another by the Archbishop of Toledo – demonstrate the increased concern of the Church regarding overindulgence, particularly during religious ceremonies (see Appendix 2 for the complete text of both edicts). Chocolate's connection to sexuality, however, has persisted, and, perhaps, added to its popularity. The literary sources associated chocolate with the underbelly of Spanish society, reminding readers that its connection to the exotic unknown made it dangerous. That same exoticism, however, also made it more desirable, and the commercial value of chocolate had only one direction in which to go: up.

CHAPTER 7

Conclusion

This book has traced the cacao bean and its derived products from the pre-Colombian era to the mid-eighteenth century on both sides of the Atlantic through chronicles, medical and religious treatises, and literary texts. From its early uses as a ceremonial drink and monetary device by Indigenous groups, to daily custom in Spain, chocolate has proven to be a versatile and universally loved consumable – even if it did not start out that way. The first interactions between Spanish conquistadors and the substance were lukewarm, at best. Many derided it for its bitter taste, or flat-out ignored it. Still, within a century of first contact between Indigenous peoples and Spanish conquistadors, it began to be imported in increasing quantities into Spain.

Although originally the main focus of this book was to consider how chocolate was portrayed in the literature of Spain during the early modern period, it became necessary to incorporate sources that extended beyond the normal chronological boundaries of 1550 and 1700. For one, it is still important to consider how the cacao bean played a central role in the lives of the Indigenous peoples of what would become the Americas, prior to any contact with Europeans, in order to understand what transference of knowledge occurred as the drink travelled across the Atlantic. Sources consulted from the eighteenth century demonstrate that there is not a hard line in the perceptions surrounding chocolate; nowhere does the questioning of its worth and legitimacy in the diets of the citizens of the Iberian Peninsula suddenly end or shift simply because one century ends and another begins.

Taking their cues from the pre-Colombian uses of cacao and chocolate, Spanish practitioners of medicine and religion began to question the value the drink had in the lives of Spaniards. The concerns regarding its effects on the health – both physical and spiritual – of the inhabitants of the Iberian Peninsula would be debated for almost two centuries, and those debates were soon played out in the literary works of the time. On the medical front, the anxieties surrounding the incorporation of this foreign product in the day-to-day life of the Spanish nobility inspired all kinds of literature, from the book of discourses *Día y noche de Madrid* by Francisco Santos, which makes note of the difficulties that those of a more "delicate character" might have upon ingesting the drink, to poems like the "Décima glosada del chocolate" that laud the drink as a cure-all elixir.

Religious authorities were much more concerned with the drink's effect on the afterlife of their parishioners. The primary debate within the Church questioned the place of chocolate within the numerous fasts that devotees were expected to take part in, and whether or not drinking chocolate imparted on the imbiber enough nutritional value to break their fast. The primary literary text analysed in chapter 4, *Santa Rosa del Perú*, incorporates chocolate into the hagiographic play written for the beatification of the first American saint, demonstrating that it is the perfect drink for supplementing the fast, while keeping her soul out of mortal danger. The play also praises chocolate for its healing properties, with the *gracioso* curing himself of a toothache through his consumption of the drink.

Aside from the medicinal and religious miracles that chocolate might perform, there are other early interpretations that have reverberations still felt today. For one, the varying qualities of chocolate from different parts of the world and the economic repercussions of these qualities began to be felt almost immediately. Chocolate from the Oaxaca region was highly sought after but also quickly became difficult to find, driving up prices and forcing consumers to mix higher-quality chocolate with that of a lower quality in order to stretch the supply further, as portrayed in *Las locas caseras*. Likewise, some preparations claimed to be made from Oaxacan beans but are clearly of a lesser origin – which can have devastating results, as the titular character of *El figurón* quickly realizes.

Another perception of chocolate that has lingered is the connection to romance and seduction. Antonio Hurtado de Mendoza wrote several poems that link chocolate to courtship, romance, and sex, claiming that "cosas tiene de amor el chocolate" ("chocolate has some of love's characteristics"; Hurtado de Mendoza 3:209; trans. RG & EC), which he goes on to elucidate to his blond interlocuter. Many a protagonist tries to woo his would-be lover through gifts of chocolate, albeit sometimes with ill effects, such as that of extreme flatulence in the interlude *La garapiña*. In spite of the potential risks, the tradition of gifting chocolate as a token of love lives on today, particularly around holidays such as Valentine's Day.

Along with its connotations of seduction, there is invariably a darker side to chocolate. Although the connection to the dark arts has its roots in the New World, it continues to be made throughout much of the literature of the seventeenth century, from Ana Caro's *Valor, agravio y mujer*, in which a concoction with chocolate as a base is given to a man as a sleeping potion, to the mixture of chocolate with grave-dirt in the short interlude *Las lenguas*, culminating in the real-life rumours that Carlos II's nickname "el hechizado," or "cursed one," came from his own mother using chocolate to poison him. Eventually the association with the New World fades, and it is Spaniards themselves who are accused of promoting a potentially dangerous magic in the satirical *Relación verdadera del gran sermón*.

Almost all of these readings of chocolate converge in the only literary piece to pay homage in its entirety to the drink, the dance interlude *Baile del chocolatero*. The first lines note the economic shortcomings of selling chocolate for a living: "Yo soy un chocolatero, / y tan vagamundo he andado / que cuando trabajo más / estoy mano sobre mano" ("I am a chocolatier, and have wandered the world over, but no matter how much I work, I live hand to mouth"; Calderón de la Barca and Moreto 196). These shortcomings are soon revealed when one of the ladies asks to purchase some of his wares, even though she states, "yo me hallo sin una blanca" ("I find myself without a single coin"; 197). Although she cannot pay, she reiterates her desire to buy some, since it is apparently the most consumed drink in the world, an assertion the chocolatier confirms. There is also some reference to the use of lesser chocolate or filler to stretch the quantity, which has a negative effect on the quality of the drink: "Muchísimo maíz tiene" ("It has a lot of corn"; 198). Of course, as noted in chapter 5, one of the gentlemen asks about the medicinal properties of the drink, but the chocolatier never really answers his question, instead turning to another intellectual concern of the day, the religious fast: "Sepa que el chocolate / le toman muchos / por burla, que dispensa / de los ayunos" ("Let it be known that many drink chocolate, and in doing so thumb their noses at the fasts"; 200). The play ends with an offering of chocolate from the author to the audience, which frightens the *chocolatero* right off the stage:

2°. Y con esto pretendo
    que el baile pase,
    pues su autor os regala
    con chocolate.
CHOCOLATERO. Bien será despedirnos
    todos conformes
    antes, que desde el patio
    no nos lo soplen. (200)

SECOND MAN. And with that I expect that the dance is over; the author will now regale you with chocolate.
CHOCOLATIER. Then it would be a good idea for us to say goodbye first, so that they cannot spit it on us from the patio.

The chocolatier knows that his product is not the best and expects a negative reaction from the audience. His concern for their reaction might sound extreme, but the audience members of the day, particularly the *mosqueteros* who occupied the patio, were known for their outbursts when they were displeased by what they saw on stage, and we can only imagine that they would react in a similar fashion if the refreshments were also off.[1]

Before beginning the major research component of this book, I assumed that I would find a clear trajectory from contact to widespread consumption. As with any historical artefact, however, chocolate proved to be less straightforward than we might believe from our modern-day perspective, since it is an almost ubiquitous product now. The inclusion of literary sources muddies the waters even further. Some of the literature seems to indicate an early, generalized knowledge of the drink, such as the fictionalized dialogue regarding the uses and effects of tobacco and chocolate, published in 1618 by Bartolomé Marradón, while other, later sources – like Juan Francisco de Tejera's *La rueda y los buñelos* (~1670s) – seem to indicate that it is still not as well known as we might expect, even in the second half of the seventeenth century.

Ultimately, what I found is a rich and varied collection of literary sources that both reflect and, at times, contradict the anxieties of conquest that can be found in the medical, religious, and other historical records of the period. Although we cannot be fully sure how much, or when, chocolate is being consumed by the various classes and regions of Iberian inhabitants, we can see that it is conspicuous enough to have been incorporated into works by well-known authors of poems, plays, short interludes, and novelas. The inclusion of the drink, particularly in theatrical performances, means that even if they were not partaking in it, a wide range of the citizenry from noble to commoner would have been aware of it, at the very least. For a drink that was disparaged by many for its bitter taste and travelled a somewhat bumpy road to acceptance by Old World inhabitants, it has endured centuries of reinvention and widespread popularity, remaining a prominent part of social gatherings, and a symbol of love, lust, gluttony, and greed, even today.

Epilogue: Chocolate Then, Chocolate Now

Although we have moved away from perceptions of chocolate's magical and medicinal properties in many ways, there are still anecdotal and folkloric beliefs in the healing power of chocolate, particularly for heartbreak. Chocolate also remains tied to romantic notions, with Valentine's Day being the third largest holiday season for chocolate sales in the United States, only outpaced by Easter and Christmas (A. Thompson). Chocolate continues to fascinate and delight us and it continues to be an important feature in literatures and cultures around the world, as can be seen by the critical success of movies like *Como agua para chocolate* (1992) and *Chocolat* (2000). It is also still very important in daily Spanish life, with many cafés and bars selling *chocolate y churros* for breakfast in the morning, and later at night as a snack or dessert.

Its connection to the conquest of the New World and the beginning of the Spanish Empire has also not been forgotten. While visiting Spain in the summer of 2018, I was invited to the theatre festival "Clásicos en Alcalá," where I attended the debut performance of *Mestiza*, a new play written by Julieta Soria and put on by the company Emilia Yagüe Producciones. The premise of the play is simple: Francisca Pizarro Yupanqui (Gloria Muñoz) is living out the end of her life in her garden in Madrid. The product of early intermarriage between a Spanish conquistador, Francisco Pizarro, and an Incan princess, Quispe Sisa, she was brought up thinking she would inherit the whole world, but instead ended up alone and impoverished, rejected by Spain's court and monarchy. She is visited by a young Tirso de Molina (Julián Ortega), who is in search of material to write about the Americas, for what will become his *Trilología de los Pizarro*. As a parting gift, in thanks for all that she has shared with him, he gives her some cacao beans, whose aroma reminds her of her youth and her mother in Peru. Muñoz then descends from the stage and distributes the beans among audience members, all the while telling her story as she moves around the theatre.

Soria's inclusion of cacao in *Mestiza* as a way to connect Pizarro back to her youth is a powerful symbol of the connection between Spain and the New World, particularly in the hands of a character whose very existence is the product of the first contact between them. Although her hybrid nature has forced her into hiding in this version of her story, it is also seen as a marker of her strength and perseverance. As she tells it to Tirso, she has moved across oceans and cultures, and has always adapted and survived, whatever circumstances she has found herself in.

Although we now live in a fully "discovered" world – there are no more new, inhabitable places to be "found," at least not on this planet – we are also living in a time of increased mobility by the most vulnerable among us. Just days after I attended the premiere of *Mestiza*, a group of rescue ships in the Aquarius aid convoy carrying 630 migrants began docking in Spain after having been rejected by various other European Union countries. The southern border of the United States has gone through periods of extreme crisis in recent times. In the public discussion held after *Mestiza*, called the "Clásicas críticas," the play was not overly well received, with critic Juan Ignacio Garcías Garzón of *ABC* and scholar Javier Huerta of the Instituto del Teatro de Madrid-UCM proclaiming it to be one-sided and too politically correct, points which they reiterate in their official blogposts for the festival. And their sentiments are not uncommon. In March of 2019,

Spain refused to recognize any wrongdoing that might have been done by conquistadors on the empire's behalf (Lafuente and Abellán). These are not long-forgotten moments; they continue to have an impact on the lives of millions today. We would do well to remember the not so distant times, when it was possibly our ancestors knocking on unknown doors. Perhaps we should revive the custom of offering any guest, expected or not, a cup of chocolate as a sign of our hospitality and welcome.

Chocolate in the Early Modern Imagination

Appendix 1 – Antonio de Colmenero Ledsma's Ingredient List

A cada cien Cacaos se le mezclan dos chiles, de los que tengo dicho, grandes que se llaman Chilpatlagua, y en lugar destos de las Indias, se pueden procurar los más anchos, y menos calientes pimientos de España. De anís un puño, orejuelas, que llaman Vinacaxtlidos, y otros dos que llaman Mecasuchil, si el vientre estuviere astrito. Y en lugar deste en España seis rosas de Alexandria en polvos. Vainilla de Campeche una, canela dos adarmes, almendras, y avellanas de cada cosa una docena, azúcar media libra. Achiote la cantidad que bastare para teñirlo todo. (8r)

For every one hundred cacao beans mix in two chilies, of those that I have mentioned, large, named "Chilpatlagua," and in place of those from the Indies, procure the widest and least spicy peppers of Spain. A handful of anise, bundles [of spices] called Vinacaxtlidos, and two more called Mecasuchil, if the stomach is off. In place of this in Spain, six powdered roses of Alexandria. One dram of vanilla from Campeche, two of cinnamon, a dozen each of almonds and hazelnuts, half a pound of sugar. Enough achiote to dye it all.

Appendix 2 – Edicts Prohibiting the Ingestion of Chocolate in the Church

Luis Manuel Fernández de Portocarrero, *Edicto en que se manda prohibir el almorzar, comer, merendar, bever, tomar chocolate, ù otros qualesquier refrescos, ò colaciones en las iglesias, capillas, hermitas, oratorios, assi publicos, como privados, y en otros lugares sagrados de nuestro arçobispado*, 1681.

Habiendo llegado a nuestra noticia el abuso irreligioso y detestable que se ha introducido en esta Corte, y otros Lugares de nuestro Arzobispado, de almorzar, comer, y merendar, beber, tomar chocolate, y otros refrescos, y colaciones (que en algunos Pueblos suelan llamar solaces) en las Iglesias, Hermitas, Capillas, Oratorios, y otros Lugares Sagrados. Y considerando la grave ofensa que en ello se hace a Dios Nuestro Señor, en desprecio de sus Templos Santos, y Lugares dedicados a su mayor veneración, y culto, como claramente nos lo enseña el Apóstol San Pablo, reprehendiendo con severidad semejantes abusos a los de Corinto en la Carta primera que los escribió, que es una de sus Epístolas Canónicas, por estas palabras: Ya no os juntáis en la Iglesia a participar de la Cena del Señor, sino venís a hacer en ella vuestras propias cenas. ¿No tenéis por ventura casas para comer, y beber? o ¿despreciáis la Iglesia Santa de Dios, comiendo, y bebiendo en ella? ˉQué os diré? y ¿qué os debo decir en exceso, y en abuso tan grave? ¿Juzgáis acaso esto digno de alabanza? porque no lo es, sino de gravísima reprehensión. I. *Corinto*. II. Y no puede la inconsideración, o inadvertencia de los que lo hacen excusarlos de culpa, siendo, como es, por si tan manifiesta la irreverencia que en esto se hace a Dios, y a sus Santos Templos, y Lugares Sagrados, como se infiere claramente de las mismas palabras, y reprehensión del Apóstol.

Mandamos a todos los Fieles de cualquier grado, y calidad que sean, no almuercen, coman, merienden, beban, ni tomen chocolate, ni otras colaciones, o refrescos, ni solaces en las Iglesias, Capillas,

Ermitas, Oratorios públicos, ni privados, ni en otros cualesquier Lugares Sagrados, ni en los Atrios, o soportales dellos, por ninguna causa, ni pretexto que tengan, pena de Excomunión mayor, en que incurran ipso facto, sin otra sentencia, ni declaración; y de toras penas a nuestro arbitrio, que se ejecutarán irremisiblemente contra los transgresores. Y debajo de las mismas penas, y censuras mandamos a todas, y cualesquier personas a cuyo cargo estuviere el gobierno y cuidado de las dichas Iglesias, Capillas, Ermitas, Oratorios públicos, o privados, y otros cualesquier Lugares Sagrados, no lo den, ni lo reciban, no lo permitan dar, ni recibir a otras personas en ninguno de los dichos Lugares, ni les consientan hacer cosa alguna contra lo que aquí por Nos mandado. Y para que mejor se guarde, y cumpla, y que ninguno pueda pretender ignorancia: Mandamos, que este nuestro Edicto se lea, y publique en las Iglesias de nuestro Arzobispado en tres días de Fiesta de precepto, al tiempo de la Misa Mayor, y cuando la mayor parte de la gente concurriere junta. Y que le fije una copia dél impresa en la Sacristía, u otro lugar de la Iglesia, que pareciere más a propósito, para que fácilmente se pueda leer, y venir a noticia de todos. Y que obligue desde su publicación, como si a cada uno de los Fieles se les hubiese notificado en su persona. Dado en Madrid a veinte y nueve de abril de 1681 años.

El Cardenal Portocarrero
    Por mandado del Cardenal mi señor.
    D. *Juan Bautista de Olavarrieta,*
        Secretario.

It has come to our attention that the ungodly and abhorrent abuse has been introduced in this court, and other places like our archbishopric, of having lunch, eating, having snacks, drinking, having chocolate, and other drinks, and collations (that in some villages are known as "solaces") in churches, shrines, sanctuaries, and other sacred places. And considering that this practice does great offence towards God our Lord, in disregarding his sacred temples, dedicated to the greatest of worships and devotion, as is clearly taught to us by Apostle Saint Paul, who apprehended with severity similar abuses to those from Corinth in the first letter that he wrote, which is one of his canonical epistles, with these words: You no longer gather in church to participate in the Lord's dinner, but rather you make your own dinner. Do you not have your own homes in which to eat, and drink? Or do you despise the Holy Church of God, eating and drinking in it? What ought I tell you? And what must I tell you in the face of such excess, and such grave abuse? Do you deem this to be worthy of worship? 1 Corinthians 2. And it can't be that the inconsideration or inadvertence of those who do it excuses them from their faults, since the irreverence is so manifest that in this is done towards God, and his Holy Temples, and sacred places, as is clearly inferred from the same words and rebuke of the Apostle.

We order all the faithful of any degree or quality that they might be, do not have lunch, eat, snack, drink, or take coffee, or any other collations or drinks, or solaces in churches, shrines, sanctuaries, public chapels, or private or any other sacred places, or in the atriums, or their porticos, for any reason, or pretext they may have, or they will incur ipso facto the punishment of major excommunication without any other sentence, or declaration; from the penalty of Mosaic Law, our judgment will be executed irremissibly against the transgressors. And under these punishments and condemnations we order everyone, and whoever is in position to be in the government and care of the churches, shrines, sanctuaries, public chapels, or private [ones], or any other sacred places, do not give to them, do not receive them, do not allow them to give or receive other people in any of the said places, or please them in doing anything against what has been ordered here. And for this law to be kept best, and followed, so no one may pretend ignorance, we order this our edict to be read and published in the churches of our archbishopric, in the three days of the festival of precept, at the time of the major Mass, and when the largest number of people is brought together; and that a copy be fixed at the sacristy, or any other place of the church, that may look to be on purpose, for it to be read easily and come as a notice to everybody, and commands from its very first publishing, as if each of the faithful was notified in person. Given on Madrid on the twenty-ninth of April of the year 1681.

Cardenal Portocarrero
By order of the Cardenal, my lord.
D. *Juan Bautista de Olavarrieta,*
Secretary. (Trans. RG & EC)

Sabo Milini, *Edicto de Don Sabo Milini, nuncio apostólico en España, prohibiendo tomar chocolate, almorzar, comer y beber en las iglesias, a cualquier clase de personas, condición y categoría,* 1681.

Habiendo llegado a noticia de nuestro muy Santo Padre Innocencio Papa Undécimo el excesivo abuso, que hay en esta Corte, y en las demás Ciudades, Villas, y Lugares destos Reinos, en tomar chocolate, y almorzar, comer, y beber en las Iglesias dellas, de que se siguen graves escándalos, e irreverencia a Dios nuestro Señor y a sus Sagrados Templos, que solo deben frecuentarse para alabarle, y pedir misericordia de nuestras culpas, y pecados con humildad y santo respeto, y que de no hacerlo así se da por muy ofendida su Divina Majestad, como se experimenta en los diversos castigos, y calamidades con que nos avisa para la enmienda, la cual deseando su Santidad con su celosa vigilancia, Nos ha encargado con su carta expresa de 24 de Noviembre del año pasado de 1680 que hagamos, que en todas las Iglesias sujetas a nuestra jurisdicción, y exemptas de la jurisdicción ordinaria, no se permita el tomar chocolate, ni almorzar, ni comer, ni beber, a cualquier género de personas, de cualquier grado o condición que sean. Por tanto, poniendo en ejecución lo mandado por su Santidad en dicha carta, mandamos a todas, y cualesquier personas, así Seglares, como Regulares, de cualquier Orden o instituto Regular, de cualquier calidad, y condición que sean exemptos de la jurisdicción ordinaria, y sujetos a la Santa Sede Apostólica, y a Nos en su nombre, que en las Iglesias, Tribunas dellas, Claustros de Conventos, ni en otras partes sagradas, exceptuando en los Conventos de Monjas los Locutorios, y los Claustros de adentro, no den, ni tomen, ni dejen tomar chocolate, ni almorzar, ni comer cosa alguna, so pena de excomunión mayor latœ sententiœ, y de privación de voz activa, y pasiva, y de suspensión de oficios, y otras penas a nuestro arbitrio, en que incurran sin otra declaración alguna, con apercibimiento, que constándonos de la contravención por informes públicos, o secretos de nuestro Ministros, o otras persona fidedignas, procederemos irremisiblemente contra los inobedientes a la ejecución de las dichas penas; y para que este nuestro Edicto se guarde, y cumpla, y no se pueda en tiempo alguno alegar ignorancia, mandamos a todos los Generales, Provinciales, Administradores de Hospitales, Rectores de Colegios, y demás Superiores de las Religiones, y a todos los demás, que son sujetos a nuestra jurisdicción, y exemptos de la jurisdicción ordinaria, en virtud de santa obediencias, que hagan luego publicar este nuestro Edicto en todos los Conventos, y Iglesias de su jurisdicción, y hagan fijar una copia del impresa en lugar publico de cada Convento, adonde todos pueden cómodamente leerla, y dentro de un mes de cómo será publicado en esta Corte, obligue a todos, como si fuera intimado a cada uno en su persona, advirtiendo, que en los Conventos de Religiosos, que no tienen lugar apartado para dar de comer a los operarios, y manuales, puedan en este caso tan solamente darles la comida en el Claustro, o en otra parte mas retirada. Dado en Madrid a treinta días del mes de Abril de 1681 años. *S. Archiep. Casarea, N. Apost. & Collect. Generalis.*

Por mandado de su Señoría Ilustrísima. Baltasar Fernández Montero.

Notice having arrived to our very Holy Father Pope Innocent XI of the excessive abuse that is in this Court, and the rest of the Cities,

Towns, and places of this realm, in taking chocolate, and having it for lunch, eating it and drinking it in the churches of these [places], which are followed by great scandals, and irreverence to God our Lord and his Sacred Temples, which must only be frequented to worship him and to ask for clemency for our faults and sins with humility and holy respect, and in not doing so offending his Divine Majesty, as the punishments and calamities that arise are so varied. As such, his Holiness with his zealous vigilance has ordered us with his expressive letter of the 24th of November of the past year of 1680 what to do, in all churches under our jurisdiction, and exempt from the ordinary jurisdiction: not to allow chocolate, or lunch, or eating, or drinking, by people, whatever class or condition they may be from. Thus, executing the mandate of his Holiness in the said letter, we order all and any people, whether secular or regular, from any class or regular institute, of any quality and condition who are exempt from ordinary jurisdiction and subject to the Holy Apostolic headquarters, and us in their name, in the churches, their tribunals, cloisters of convents, and all other sacred places, excluding in the convents of nuns the visiting rooms, and the cloisters inside, do not give, do not take, do not let them have chocolate, or lunch, or eat anything, or they will suffer from immediate major excommunication without sentencing, and of the loss of an active voice, or passive, and of suspension of trades, and other punishments, by our discretion, which will be made without any declaration, with warning, and they will be ascertained by public or secret reports from our ministers, or other trustworthy people, we will execute irremissibly against the disobedient the said punishments; and for this our Edict is to be kept in all convents and churches of its jurisdiction, and a printed copy is to be fixed in a public place of every convent, where everyone can comfortably read it, warning each person that in the convents of those who are religious, not to have a place set aside to feed the workers and manual labourers; they may only in this case give them food in the cloister, or any part that's farther removed [from the actual church]. Given in Madrid at thirty days of the month of April of the year 1681. Archipelago Casarea, Apostolic Nuncio and General Aid.

By decree of his Excellency Baltasar Fernández Montero. (Trans. RG & EC)

Notes

Introduction

1 In the sixteenth century, Spain developed a "sistema de castas" or caste system to help explain the racial make-up of the new generations that would come out of the intermarriage between Spaniards, Indigenous peoples, and African slaves in the New World. *Criollo* or "Creole," within this system, was the name given to descendants of two Spanish parents, born in the New World.

2 Note that entries of Spanish names that begin with "de" are alphabetized in the works cited in the Spanish fashion. For example, Antonio de Nebrija will appear as Nebrija, Antonio de.

3 Although Fernández-de-Pinedo is looking more closely at a slightly later period, she claims that chocolate drinking was as much a "symbol of respectability" by the mid-eighteenth century as "dressing fashionably and showing off particular objects such as table clocks or porcelain and gourds" (307).

1. Pre-Columbian Conceptions of Chocolate

1 For more on the use of the incorporation of pre-Columbian references, particularly in the context of evangelization, see Sergio Romero.

2 Alejo Venegas was a well-known author and academic in the first half of the sixteenth century, whose writings – particularly *Primera parte de las diferencias de libros que ay en el universo* – influenced contemporary thought on the validity of knowledge and forms of writing. For more on this and Venegas's connections to the Americas, see Mignolo 69–76.

3 Michela E. Craveri notes that *pataxte* is a Nahuatl word that refers to a plant within the cacao species (*Theobroma bicolor*), while "cacao" itself

refers to the more commonly known cacao plant *Theobroma cacao* (133n).
Coe and Coe, however, explain that *Theobroma bicolor* does not produce
cacao but rather that the *pataxte* can be used on its own as a drink or
as an inexpensive dilution to stretch out the costlier chocolate drink, but
cannot be considered a direct source of cacao (25). Nathaniel Bletter and
Douglas C. Daly, on the other hand, claim that it is in fact the *Theobroma
bicolor* seeds that were the most likely of all the *Theobroma* species to have
been used as a food early on: "*T. bicolor* is the only species whose seeds
were likely a traditional foodstuff in prehistoric Amazonia, and these are
roasted like a nut without fermentation and in no way resemble cacao in
their flavor, chemistry, or South American uses" (36). See table 2.2 of their
article "Cacao and Its Relatives in South America" for more uses of *pataxte*
by various Indigenous groups throughout the Americas, including the
mixture of the seeds with those of cacao for a chocolate known as "madre
del cacao" (49–58). See Johanna Kufer and Cameron L. McNeil for an
explanation of the botanical differences between *T. cacao* and *T. bicolor*, as
well as modern uses of the seed and its fruit for foods and drinks.

4 Although, as Timothy Knowlton points out, the incantations of the *Ritual
of the Bacabs* were primarily written down so that they might be performed,
rather than read, he also demonstrates that the manuscript can be used
to understand the connections – and disconnections – between speech,
alphabetic writing, and graphic representations in Maya literacy. See his
article "Literacy and Healing: Semiotic Ideologies and the Entextualization
of Colonial Maya Medical Incantations" for more.

5 Bolles notes that the Yucatec word *tancas* has a variety of interpretations,
but he opts for "seizure," because of the descriptions given in the text of
an illness characterized by "restlessness, irritability, frenzied excitement, a
kind of madness, heightened eroticism and fever, nausea," while Roys varied
his word choice between "seizure" and "spasm" (Bolles 1n). Bolles's choice
gives a more modern interpretation of such an affliction.

6 Although the short- and long-term effects of chocolate might have seemed
magical or mysterious to both the Indigenous and Spanish imbibers of
the early modern period, Bletter and Daly demonstrate that the majority
of the medicinal uses can be broken down into five categories: "stimulant
or treatment for fatigue; high-calorie food for weight gain; external and
internal emollient; antiseptic; and snakebite remedy," and that those effects
can all be explained by actual chemical properties present in the *Theobroma*
family of plants (62–3).

7 Dr Francisco Hernández, in his 1615 four-volume set on the plants and
medicines found in Mexico, states that "la que dicen cacahuaxochitl o flor
del cacao, una yerba, que tiene las hojas de figura de corazón, los rallos de

a palma, las flores purpureas" ("The cachoaxóchitl or cacaoatl flower is an herb that has heart-shaped leaves, stems a span long, purple flowers"; 125v; Varey 146). This description is vastly different from that of the Badianus Manuscript, in which Emmart's notes explain: "The illustration of the cacauaxochitl ... represents a plant with yellow flowers borne in the young terminal branches, and with fruit of a light cinnamon brown color. The leaves are oblanceolate and are characteristic of the species *Theobroma augustifolium* DC. This is one of the important cacao plants. Standley reports that it is grown especially in the State of Chiapas in the region of Socomusco [*sic*], which has long been famous for its chocolate" (Emmart 311n). Thus the flowers described by Hernández and those portrayed in the Badianus Manuscript and annotated by Emmart are markedly dissimilar flowers from different regions (although not mentioned in the original text by Hernández, the translators note that the cacahoaxóchitl of which he speaks is grown in "Yancuitlan in Upper Mixteca" – presumably today's Yanhuitlan, approximately halfway between the cities of Oaxaca and Tehuacán in Oaxaca state) (Varey 146).

2. Encountering Chocolate: What Is It Good For?

1 Although one might argue that some of their accounts border on the fantastical, it is their intent, rather than any potential misinterpretations of the New World, that I am commenting on.
2 The actual evidence of this supposition by Alvar is scarce. The footnote to his edition simply states "*Un grano en una escudilla. Creo que se refiere al 'cacao'*" ("*A bean in a bowl.* I believe this refers to the 'cacao' bean"; Colón, *Diario* 167n, emphasis in the original). Varela Bueno only points to Alvar as a source for this information (Colón, *Textos y documentos* 94n). It is entirely possible that it was some other grain or bean that was made into a drink, or that it was in fact chocolate, but without further corroboration it is impossible to know either way.
3 "Columbus" in Spanish is "Colón," and thus any documents cited in Spanish will show up in the Works Cited under that name rather than the anglicized version.
4 Although his text was not published until the nineteenth century, we know it was widely read and cited by a number of other prominent historians of the sixteenth and seventeenth centuries (Díaz Balsera 111).
5 For more information on the use of chocolate in festivities, see Durán, *Historia* 1:338 (Heyden and Horcasitas trans. 189); as a welcome for honoured guests, see 1:348 (trans. 191); as a part of sacrificial rituals, see 1:352 (trans. 194); and in funerals, see 1:305–7 (trans. 176–7).

6 David Carrasco does not include parts of this selection in his 2008 translation, but rather glosses over the implications made by Díaz del Castillo regarding the women who served Montezuma and the choice of the Spaniards not to look into it, stating only that they "served this drink to him with great reverence" (ch. 16). It seems odd that Carrasco would suppress this innuendo, given that earlier in the same chapter he includes references to Montezuma's many mistresses and two legitimate wives, demonstrating that Montezuma's relations with multiple women were clearly known.

7 Acuña is careful to note that his attribution is purely speculative but does demonstrate that the letter bears remarkable similarities to the last chapter of Díaz del Castillo's *Historia verdadera* (264).

8 For more on the debated identity – and even possible non-existence – of the Anonymous Conquistador, see Jesús Bustamante's introductory study "La atracción de lo raro y peregrino" in his side-by-side Italian-Spanish version of the *Relación*.

9 Although the *entremés* was not printed until the eighteenth century, Tejera's death in 1678 means it was written before that date.

3. Chocolate-Covered Commerce: How Chocolate Came into Popularity in the Old World

1 Although this book deals primarily with the "early modern" period of Spain, normally delineated as occurring between 1550 and 1700, the ongoing debates, legal cases, and royal decrees that continued beyond the end of the seventeenth century will also be included to demonstrate the persistence of the drink and the controversy surrounding it, particularly in terms of the economics of its importation and distribution.

2 Although "carga" can refer generally to a load (as on a ship or in a cart), there is the possibility that here it refers to another definition of "carga" that we find in the *Diccionario de autoridades*: "Cierta porción de granos, que en Castilla son cuatro fanegas. Díjose así por ser el peso que regularmente puede llevar una béstia" ("A certain portion of grains (or seeds), which in Castile equals four bushels. They call it that because it is the weight that can generally be carried by a beast [ox]").

3 My thanks to anonymous reviewer number three for pointing out this potential reading and directing me to Janine Gasco's work.

4 Cacao beans and their derived drink are thought to have been first introduced to Spain in 1544 by a group of Mayan nobles, and brought by Dominican friars to the court for Prince Philip, but general shipments of chocolate did not start arriving through Spanish ports until 1585 (Coe and Coe 130–3).

5 One early exception to this can be found in Cervantes's "La gitanilla" (1613), which is set in Castile and follows the life of a young gypsy woman who dances and sings for money. The word *cacao* appears in the discourse of an old man who is trying to pass on his knowledge of his trade – pickpocketing – to a younger man who is new to the family business: "El toque está [en] no acabar acoceando el aire en la flor de nuestra juventud, y a los primeros delitos, que el mosqueo de las espaldas, ni el apalear el agua en las galeras, no lo estimamos en un cacao" ("The trick is (in) not wasting the flower of our youth on our first offences, but to have our backs lashed, or rowing the rough waters in the galleys, we do not mind it even one cacao bean"; "Novela de la gitanilla" 105; trans. RG & EC). Other translations might change "un cacao" to "a bit" or "a lick" to be more idiomatically English, but we have opted to leave it here for the sake of our present purposes. This is a particularly interesting employment of the New World good, given that Cervantes does not mention chocolate in any other form in any of his writings.

6 In spite of being officially published in 1620, rights were granted to the author in 1613 and 1614, making this *comedia* in prose likely one of the earliest literary texts to mention chocolate.

7 Oaxaca, Guatemala, and Campeche are all regions where chocolate grows abundantly, with that of Oaxaca being considered the best quality.

8 The very first *comedia* dedicated to the conquest of the New World, *El nuevo mundo descubierto por Cristóbal Colón*, has an allegorical scene in which Religion takes Idolatry and the Devil to the court of Providence to fight over who should rule over the New World and its Indigenous peoples.

9 W.A. Shaw tells us that the *real* of eight was renamed *escudo de plata* in 1686 with a new value of ten *reales* of new silver (330), while *Diccionario de autoridades* gives the following definition: "Se llama también cierta especie de moneda, por estar en ella grabado el escudo de las armas del Rey o Príncipe soberano, y por excelencia se entiende la que es de oro. En España por escudo absolutamente se significa el que vale la mitad de un doblón. En los Reinos de Castilla y León hay también escudos de plata y de vellón: el de plata tiene de valor ocho reales de plata antigua, y es lo mismo que un real de a ocho de dicha plata, y el de vellón tiene de valor diez reales de vellón" ("It is also the name of a certain kind of coin, for on it is engraved the emblem or arms of the sovereign King or Prince, and by excellence it is understood that it is made of gold [although in the case of the *escudo de plata*, the material would be silver]. In Spain by 'absolute escudo' they are referring to a coin that is worth half a 'doblón.' In the kingdoms of Castilla and León there are *escudos* of silver and of vellon: the silver one has the value of eight *reales* of old silver, and the same as a *real*

of eight of said silver, and the vellon has the value of ten *reales* of vellon";
trans. RG & EC).

10 For more on the connection between the Indigenous women as
representatives of Otherness in this play, see Glenda Y. Nieto-Cuebas's
"Amazons in the Indies or Witches in the Amazon?"

11 A *botillería* was a shop that would sell cold drinks and other concoctions.
For more information, see M. Herrero García, *La vida española en el siglo
XVII* 1:165–6.

12 I have chosen to translate "auroras y sorbetes" as "additives" to avoid
confusion. *Aurora* can refer to the dawn of a new day, but it was also the
name of a drink made of almond milk and cinnamon, while *sorbete* was a
drink made of fruit juices mixed with sugar (*Diccionario de autoridades*).
Given the already complex nature of the concoction – and that almond milk
and cinnamon are still added in later – I felt it best to remove the added
explanation from the translated verses.

13 According to Shaw, the *real* of eight was being issued after a great economic
reform in 1497 as the equivalent of ten *reales*, which would complicate the
math. However, he also tells us that by 1680, through a series of reductions
and reorderings of currency in Spain, the *real* of eight was worth twenty-
nine *reales* of bullion, and thus two *reales* of eight would make fifty-eight
reales of bullion, a much closer sum to that requested of Don Gil in *La
garapiña*. See Shaw 329.

14 According to Fernández-de-Pinedo's calculations, sugar was imported at
a rate of 25.83 pounds per year, chocolate at 17.63 pounds, and cacao at
16.76 pounds. The category of "sweets" also had a high rate of import,
particularly among the lower classes, at a total of 46.69 pounds per year, 24
of which were imported by the "middle lower class" alone, and which were
mainly "crystallised fruit made with sugar" (299).

15 This disdain is made explicit, although possibly sarcastically, in Quiñones de
Benavente's *Don Gaiferos* (1643), when Melisendra attempts to deride the
advances of the title character: "Plegue Dios que un indiano te maltrate /
haciéndote beber el chocolate / y algún sucio bellaco / por fuerza te haga
estornudar tabaco" ("May God send an *indiano* that mistreats you by
making you drink chocolate, and some dirty villain, that makes you inhale
tobacco by force"; 611; trans. RG & EC). Melisendra's protestations are
really compliments in disguise, taking actions that a woman would likely
welcome – the chocolate certainly, the tobacco perhaps less so – and making
them sound objectionable.

16 Amado Doblas cites this work as "El soletero [*sic*] indiano" and gives
the authorship an earlier date of 1648, stating that it was printed in a
compilation called *Jardín ameno*, and then later printed in *Pensil ameno*

(1691) as "El calcatero [*sic*] indiano" ("En el V centenario I" 282n), which
is the volume that I am citing, as I could not find a reference to the earlier
volume elsewhere. According to Tania de Miguel Magro, this is in part
because Amado Doblas miscites both the date, which should be 1684 not
1648, and the title, which should be "El soltero indiano" (*El calcetero
indiano*). To add to the confusion, the online catalogue for the Biblioteca
Nacional de España erroneously lists this *entremés* in the contents of *Pensil
ameno* as "Del cabretero indiano." De Miguel Magro has also informed me
that there is a *suelta* (similar to an English quarto) of this play held by the
Biblioteca del Instituto del Teatro de Barcelona, and it is also included in the
volume *Entremeses varios escritos por don Gil de Armesto y Castro* (1646),
which can also be found at the Biblioteca Nacional de España (*El calcetero
indiano*). These various editions with their erroneous titles, dates, etc. also
make it difficult to put an exact date on the composition of the text.

17 De Miguel Magro notes that the name of the *gracioso* in this play, Tarugo,
has two meanings, both of which this Tarugo's character contradicts: the
first is dumb, while our Tarugo is actually quite intelligent; the other is
a sort of nail used to keep doors and windows closed, while our Tarugo
is able to gain entrance to a locked-up home ("A Study of Women's
Intelligence" 96).

18 Chocolate was gaining acceptance and popularity, while tobacco was still
considered quite sinful, so the comparison here is perhaps alluding to a
darker take on the popularity of chocolate. For more information on the
differences and similarities in attitudes towards chocolate and tobacco, see
Marcy Norton, *Sacred Gifts, Profane Pleasures.*

19 A short interlude entitled *El sordo* (1668), written by Quirós just a
few years after *No puede ser*, also indicates that chocolate was seen as
something that should be offered to guests upon their arrival at one's
home. Preparing her house for the arrival of her suitor, the titular deaf
man, Doña Endrina indicates all the preparations that need to be made
to her servant, including "y el chocolate a punto en la cocina / sepa don
Lesmes quién es doña Endrina" ("and the chocolate ready to boil in
the kitchen, so that Don Lesmes knows exactly who Doña Endrina is";
148r). Of course, the rest of the play is just the two potential spouses
misunderstanding each other because of Lesmes' lack of hearing, and they
never do get to try the chocolate, although they do end up engaged to be
married, somehow.

20 Although the Biblioteca Nacional de España catalogue lists Francisco de
Rojas Zorilla as the author of the volume in which this *entremés* appears,
there are a number of authors attached to the four *comedias* and various
interludes therein. Agapita Jurado Santos names Matos Fragoso as the

author of this particular *entremés* in *Obras teatrales derivadas de las novelas cervantinas* (205).

21 While not explicit about economic value, María de Zayas makes one mention of chocolate in the introduction to her second compilation of *novelas*. The date of publication, 1647, would place it right in the middle of this period of relative quiet, making her comment that chocolate is a friend that one can find anywhere all the more poignant (120). For more in-depth analysis of this quote, see chapter 6.

22 It is difficult to place this *entremés* temporally, as Calderón never had his own interludes printed, but the manuscript conserved in the Biblioteca Nacional de España (MS 15596) does give a clue as to when it might have been written or, at least, performed. On the back of the last page there is a note from Jerónimo Peñarroja that reads, "he visto este entremés que no me parece mal, esos señores son los que han de contentarse que yo en esto no supongo" ("I have seen the interlude and it does not seem bad to me; those gentlemen are the ones who must be happy with it, for I have nothing to say on the matter"; trans. Rodríguez in "Editing Theater" 100), followed by a list of character names and actors. Evangelina Rodríguez and Antonio Tordera do an excellent job highlighting the close relationship between Peñarroja and Calderón, demonstrating the likelihood that the inscription and cast list on the back of *La rabia* can be linked to possible performances sometime after 1671, with the most likely dates being between 1677 and 1679 (*Calderón y la obra corta dramática* 156–8). This also coincides with my analysis that the literary sources from the latter half of the seventeenth century demonstrate a more widespread use and acceptance of chocolate as a commercial product.

23 Although published in a volume in the early 1700s, this *entremés*, and all de Olmedo's other work, had to have been produced before his death in 1682. The exact date of completion is unknown, but we know that this *entremés*, along with two others, *La dama toro* and *El sacristan chinchilla*, and several of his *bailes* were performed at a festival in Valencia in 1665.

24 The *piedra bezal* or *piedra bezoar* is a stone created in the stomach of mountain goats who often eat foods that are hard on their digestive system, first found in New Spain. As Gustavo Curiel points out, it was believed to have magical properties during the colonial era, for its ability to cure all kinds of poisons and other illnesses (295).

25 It is difficult to know the date of writing/performance. The manuscript in the Biblioteca Nacional de España (MS 14782) is listed in the catalogue as "between 1601 and 1700," while the database *Manos teatrales* confirms that it is a copy that pertains to the hand of Juan Francisco Sáenz de Tejera, who died in 1710 and seems to have been most active during the latter part

of the seventeenth century. Again, this later time period would fit with the analytical framework laid out here.

26 *Rosca* is a circular bread or cake (*Diccionario de autoridades*).

27 The King's penchant for chocolate and the ways in which it is used against him will be discussed in chapter 6.

28 Although this particular document is not dated, the documents surrounding it in the same packet are dated 1718 and 1719, making this the best approximation at a date.

29 De la Cruz also includes other New World products, such as tobacco, in several plays, and joins his predecessors in including cacao as part of a crude joke: "INDIANO. ... con el mejor cacao / de Caracas y Moxos. / DOÑA INOCENCIA. ¿Qué estáis diciendo, Don Mauro, / de Mocos? ¡Qué porquería!" ("INDIANO. ... with the best cacao from Caracas and Moxos. DOÑA INOCENCIA. What are you talking about, Don Mauro, from snot? How disgusting!"; "Las dos viuditas" 312). This time the confusion comes not from the word *cacao* itself, which is too well known by the late eighteenth century to lend itself to wordplay, but rather from the product's region of origin, Moxos, in modern-day Bolivia, which the innocent young widow mistakes for the Spanish word for mucus or snot, "mocos."

4. Chocolate in the Church: Ecclesiastical Debates on Chocolate and Fasting

1 I have chosen not to translate *jícara*, although one might do so as *gourd*, given that such fruits were the first carved to serve as cups from which chocolate was drunk. The *jícara* underwent its own transformation as it crossed the Atlantic, eventually being made out of the finest of materials such as ceramic, silver, and gold, and was specifically for use with chocolate.

2 Earle notes that there were two vices to which colonialists would frequently point to demonstrate their superiority over Indigenous groups. The first, expounded upon here, is, of course, cannibalism. The second, which is also connected to the religious question, is alcohol intolerance. It was thought that the Indigenous constitution could not handle alcohol, and Indigenous people were thus sometimes prevented from, or denied outright, the opportunity to partake in the sacrament of the eucharist where wine was involved ("Spaniards, Cannibals, and the Eucharist" 85). This echoes claims we saw previously from early colonial sources that chocolate might not function well in Spanish bodies, assertions that would be repeated, as will be seen in the next chapter, by the medical community in Spain.

3 The two groups were perhaps not so dissimilar as early modern theologians such as Pinelo would have liked to assume. Earle's chapter on cannibalism and the eucharist does a very good job of breaking down the hypocrisy of

the European perspective on cannibalism and provides examples of Spanish and European cannibalism, as well as dissecting the ritual of the eucharist and its connections to sacrifice and cannibalism, particularly in the Catholic Church. For more, see "Spaniards, Cannibals, and the Eucharist."

4 This book, however, only includes two recipes that reference the bird: the first, "To bake a Turkie," gives brief instructions on how to roast a turkey, much as you would any other fowl; the second is for a sauce to accompany the roasted meat. There is no mention of it specifically in relation to stews.

5 Although this book was not published until the nineteenth century, we know that it was written prior to the author's death in 1631, and was likely written in the last decade of his life, when he also published several other volumes dedicated to the Spanish language, as well as its connections to Greek and Latin (Mir v–vi).

6 The *molinillo* was a Spanish invention, as Amado Doblas explains. Prior to using this tool, the Indigenous preparers of chocolate would create the much-desired foam by pouring the chocolate back and forth between vessels, sometimes at a great height ("En el V centenario I" 266).

7 Antonio de Pereda's *Still Life with an Ebony Chest* was painted in Spain in 1652. The image collects together objects and commodities from both sides of the Atlantic, demonstrating, as Anne Gerritsen and Giorgio Riello explain, that these are "not just things with social lives [playing on Arjun Appadurai's *The Social Life of Things*], but with global trajectories" (3). Chocolate and the implements used to concoct the drink play a prominent role in the painting, which corresponds to their increasing importance in the social lives of Spaniards.

8 Gascón claims that this was not only a nutritional or spiritual issue, but an economical one as well: "Economically there was much at stake in the decision; a censuring of chocolate by the church would certainly affect the cacao trade, which generally benefited Spanish immigrant merchants and traders more than it did Creoles" (48).

9 For more information on the use of cacao on the South American continent, see, for example, the work of Sonia Zarrillo et al., "The Use and Domestication of Theobroma Cacao during the mid-Holocene in the Upper Amazon." I would like to thank anonymous reviewer number three for pointing me to this source.

10 Gascón argues that the play itself is not particularly evocative of the New World in terms of characterization or linguistic markers. It is certainly a play set in the New World but written in such a way as to be overtly accessible to the Spanish audience, using symbolic exoticism to titillate the audience while removing any real connection to Santa Rosa's life and surroundings (Gascón 45).

5. Chocolate: A Prescription for Health?

1 In an article for the *Journal of Nutrition*, six academics from diverse disciplines, including nutrition, anthropology, genetics, and translation, put together an extensive list of all the "positive claims and uses" attributed to chocolate in the early modern period to the end of the nineteenth century. These claims range from the benign ("warmth: increases") to the reparation of all of the major organs. Other fascinating claims include the belief that it would stave off the growth of white hair, increase sexual desire, and reduce violence (Dillinger et al. 2061S–2063S).

2 In spite of the ongoing debates, it is interesting to note that it is in a medical treatise by the "Protomédico de las Indias" Francisco Hernández de Toledo, translated into Spanish (the original being in Latin) and printed in 1615 – but written earlier, given his death in 1587 – that we find the first recorded use of the word *chocolate*, instead of *cacahuatl* or *cacao* (*Cuatro libros* A2).

3 The French translation (*Du chocolat: dialogue entre un medecin, un indien & un bourgeois*) has survived far better than the original version and it is thus that I am citing here from the French copy conserved in the Biblioteca Nacional de España. The only remaining copy of the Spanish version is currently housed in the Museo Galileo in Florence, Italy, according to WorldCat. All translations of the French to English for this book have been provided by Bridget Pupillo, PhD.

4 The "Décima glosada" as it appears here is published in Cortijo Herraiz's 1729 *Discurso apologético médico astronómico*, which offers an explanation of the influence of the heavenly bodies on human health, as well as an examination of the medicinal uses of chocolate. It also appears in an unglossed form in 1759, with some very minor changes to lines 1, 8, and 9, which read in the latter version as "es regalo universal ... que (si acaso le tomaron) / con su eficacia lograron ..." ("it is a universal gift ... that (if they were to drink it) / with its efficacy they would achieve ..."; *Poesías satíricas varias* H14). Francisco Aguilar Piñal, in his *Indice de las poesías publicadas en los periódicos españoles del siglo XVIII*, lists the poem as being published in 1772 in the *Diario Curioso de Barcelona*, volume 2, number 156 (124).

5 Given that the legend of the fountain of youth, with its ties to the New World, was still considered possible, if not plausible, in the late sixteenth and early seventeenth centuries, the idea that chocolate could be an elixir of youth would be in line with the connection of all New World goods to the exotic, unknown Other.

6 According to Colmenero, the unnamed doctor's purportedly wrong conclusion was to find chocolate "opliativo, por ser el cacao frío, y seco"

("obstructive, given that cacao is cold, and dry"; 1r). Although he refrains from revealing his own conclusions so early on, he does say that he must correct this misunderstanding, since anyone who knows how to use the cacao bean properly, and with moderation, will find it a most healthy supplement.

7 "Impinguan" appears to come from the Italian verb "impinguare," meaning "to fatten" or "to enrich."

8 Although there is no known surviving copy of his *Libro en el cual se trata del chocolate, que provechos haga y si es bebida saludable o no*, as noted in the second volume of *Iberian Books/Libros Ibéricos*, a large portion of it is conserved by extensive citation in Leon Pinelo's *Questión moral: si el chocolate quebranta el ayuno eclesiástico*. Likewise, a long passage on the origins and benefits of chocolate when mixed with the correct ingredients is cited in volume 4 of the *Historia bibliográfica de la medicina española*, compiled by Antonio Hernández Morejón and published posthumously in 1846.

9 The date of writing must be at least six years prior to the known date of publication, as Benavente died in 1651.

10 There is even some indication that tobacco was already noted for its potential health issues. In Marradón's dialogue, the Indian and the Doctor make reference on a few occasions to tobacco and its potential issues. The Indian specifically asks for more information about chocolate's relationship with tobacco: "Je vous supplie dites moi si le *Chocolat* est aussi méchant & aussi mal sain que le *Tabac*?" ("I beg you to tell me if *Chocolate* is just as evil and unhealthy as *Tobacco*?"; trans. Pupillo 172–3, emphasis in the original).

11 The entire *Entremés de la constreñida* is a disjointed series of statements made by Pedro, mostly about his sister, which the doctor to whom he speaks cannot follow, especially when the story twists and turns so rapidly, with Pedro making errors and missteps more often than not. In one instance he tells the doctor that his sister is twenty-seven years old, in another twenty-seven months. His narration is suspect – not unusual for the genre – so the medical validity of his claim here is also questionable at best.

12 See the Conclusion to this book for an analysis of this play as the culmination of all of these different influences on chocolate in the popular imagination.

13 Much as in the case of *Santa Rosa*, it is thought that Moreto had a co-author for *La fuerza del natural*, Gerónimo de Cáncer, but only some publications of the play name Cáncer as the secondary author.

14 "Cordellate" actually translates more closely to "grosgrain," an early modern cloth, similar to corduroy, but usually made of silk. The joke is somewhat lost in translation, as the homonymic quality between *chocolate* and *cordellate* in Spanish does not exist in the English words.

6. Sinfully Delicious: The Darker Side of Chocolate

1 This *gracioso* by the name of Chocolate is not the only one, or even the first. Pedro Calderón de la Barca's 1657 *Gustos y disgustos no son más que imaginación* also has a *gracioso* named Chocolate, as discussed in chapter 3.

2 Note that although his poems were not printed until the last decade of the seventeenth century, Hurtado de Mendoza died in 1644, and his work would have been written at best some fifty years before the volume appeared.

3 Although this might have been the general consensus in Spain, John Bristol and Matthew Restall have demonstrated that women of all backgrounds – racial, socioeconomic, etc. – in the New World were involved in the procuring, making, and distributing of love-potions, and in fact it was practitioners of African descent that were most likely to be denounced and prosecuted by the Inquisition, even though their services were often procured by women of Spanish lineage (161).

4 I am citing the 1664 version, which has been attributed to Avellaneda by Amado Doblas ("En el V centenario I" 273).

5 Likewise, Bristol and Restall demonstrate that chocolate was employed both on its own and as a mask for other ingredients in love-potions that were used in Mexico and Yucatan throughout the seventeenth century. The ingredients hidden in chocolate varied from the innocuous (flowers and water from special vessels) to the repellent (sweat, blood, hair, etc. from the seducer). See "Potions and Perils," 162.

6 Putting an exact date on this interlude is difficult, even though Amado Doblas cites it as circa 1670 ("En el V centenario II" 338), and there is a manuscript listed in the catalogue of the Biblioteca Nacional de España with the same title and author, with the date 1674 (MSS/16768). However, this does not appear to be the same interlude at all, and does not include this passage, or, indeed, any mention of chocolate whatsoever. As with *La boda de Juan Rana*, the *entremés* cited here is also attributed to Gerónimo de Cáncer in Zafra, *Floresta de entremeses y rasgos del ocio, a diferentes asuntos, de bailes y mogigangas* (1691), and these two *entremeses* match exactly, line for line. There is another version attributed to Calderón in a volume dated 1670–7, which contains a similar passage, but it varies significantly from the copy cited here – which is the digital edition on cervantesvirtual.com, created from a publication without date printed in Valencia, the original of which can be found in the Library of Menéndez Pelayo. This same play is also printed in *Entremeses varios ahora nuevamente recogidos de los mejores ingenios de España* with an attribution given to Calderón. This version, which was printed in Zaragoza,

is without a date, but is thought to have been printed circa 1650. Some of the confusion may come from the fact that MSS/16768 appears to have been mislabelled as a Calderón play and may actually be the version by Cáncer. Although the original hand lists it as *Entremés de las lenguas de Calderón*, another hand has written a title page with the name Cáncer and date 1674, as well as added "de Cáncer" to the top of the first page. More work would have to be done to determine the origin and authorship of the various versions of this *entremés*, some of which vary vastly, while others seem to have many similarities but have perhaps been edited and/or added to over time.

7 Although Galen's theories had begun to fall out of favour with the European medical community, he was still considered a legitimate source of medicinal knowledge and was taught in the curriculum at several universities in Spain until the late seventeenth century (Earle, *The Body of the Conquistador* 33).

8 Of course, we know, as Mary Elizabeth Perry points out, that even women who were accused of healing via magic were condemned by the Inquisition as witches, so, negative connotation or no, the connection to sorcery or witchcraft would automatically make chocolate a dangerous good, particularly in Spain (31).

9 González Quiroz theorizes that the author behind the *Relación verdadera del gran sermón* was not only a Sephardic Jew living in Amsterdam but specifically Abraham Gómez de Silviera, originating from Portugal. For more on this theory, see the section of the Introduction of her edited edition of the work titled "Un judío hispano tras el autor anónimo," 65–86.

10 Commenting on a citation regarding the heavy use and importation of chocolate by the Jesuits, Nadia Fernández-de-Pinedo remarks, "It should not be forgotten that chocolate was also the ideal drink to mask poison" (310n). It is a surprising remark to make in conjunction with the religious order, and Fernández-de-Pinedo makes no further reference to it, leaving readers to come to their own conclusions. Still, it is an indication of how closely the thick, strongly flavoured drink was tied to poisoning at the time.

11 The *arbitristas* were a group of reformers who were looking to ameliorate the underperforming Spanish economy of the late seventeenth century.

12 The reference to Cervantes's masterpiece, *El ingenioso hidalgo don Quijote de la Mancha*, is employed much in the same way that the *indianos* of *El mayorazo figura* and *La villana de Vallecas* use chocolate: to prove knowledge of a place they have once been, that will add weight to their authority about said place. Although the manuscript is anonymous, this reference points to someone who was at least aware of cultural and literary touchstones of the day.

13 For more on Hurtado de Mendoza's involvement in the court and the appearance of food and sex in his poetry, see González's article "Alimento y mujer en un poema de Antonio Hurtado de Mendoza."

14 The publication of the *Desengaños amorosos* coincides closely with a declaration by the Marquis de Cadereyta, Viceroy of New Spain in 1638, requesting that anyone hiding cacao should bring it forward or face a penalty. It appears that the ability to control chocolate – or lack thereof – is a concern throughout the empire. See Díez de Aux de Armendáriz, *Sobre depósito de cacao en la alhóndiga* in the Archivo Histórico Nacional.

15 Mariana de Carvajal y Saavedra, another early modern female writer – less known, and perhaps not as ingenious as Zayas or Caro – also includes a reference to the chocolate served to guests in a set-up similar to that of Zaya's frame story: a group of friends come together and tell each other stories in *Navidades de Madrid y noches entretenidas, en ocho novelas* (1663). In Carvajal y Saavedra's version, the guests are offered chocolate at both the beginning and end of their evening, but, aside from setting the scene slightly, there is little that it adds either to the story itself or to the analysis here at hand.

16 "No le conozca Galván" is a refrain from the time period that refers to something or someone who is unrecognizable (Martín Sánchez 517).

17 Agustín Moreto rewrites this play as *La ocasión hace al ladrón*, much of it word for word, only removing some longer monologues and making an occasional change to the dialogue, but the plot and large swaths of verse, particularly of the first and second acts, are almost completely untouched. This includes the questions posed here by Agudo (known in Moreto's version as Beltrán) to ascertain the imposter's status as an *indiano*.

Conclusion

1 See, for example, John T. Cull's "'Ese paso está ya hecho" for more information on the behaviour of theatrical audiences in the early modern period.

Works Cited

Acosta, José de. *Historia natural y moral de las Indias, en que se tratan de las cosas notables del cielo, elementos, metales, plantas y animales dellas; y los ritos, y ceremonias, leyes y gobierno de los indios.* Edited by Edmundo O'Gorman, Fondo de Cultura Económica, 1962.

Acuña, René. "Fragmento inédito de una carta atribuible a Bernal Díaz del Castillo." *Estudios de historia novohispana*, vol. 17, 1997, pp. 263–71.

Aguado, Simón, and Catalina Buezo. "Los niños de la Rollona y lo que pasa en las calles." *La mojiganga dramática: De la fiesta al teatro, II*, vol. 2, Edition Reicheberger, 2005, pp. 141–56.

Aguilar Piñal, Francisco. *Índice de las poesías publicadas en los periódicos españoles del siglo XVIII.* CSIC, 1981.

Aguilar-Moreno, Manuel. "The Good and Evil of Chocolate in Colonial Mexico." McNeil, pp. 273–88.

Albala, Ken. *Food in Early Modern Europe.* Greenwood P, 2003.

Amado Doblas, María Isabel. "En el V centenario del descubrimiento del cacao: El chocolate en la literatura del Siglo de Oro (I)." *Isla de Arriarán*, vol. 20, 2002, pp. 265–82.

– "En el V centenario del descubrimiento del cacao: El chocolate en la literatura del Siglo de Oro (II)." *Isla de Arriarán*, vol. 21, 2003, pp. 337–60.

Aponte, Diego de. *Carta de Diego de Aponte a su mujer, dándole cuenta del estado del pleito con el tuerto, de haber tenido noticias de estar preñada su hija Catalina, y de la dificultad de encontrar chocolate en la corte, pues hace dos años que no llegan galeones.* 22 March 1627. Archivo Histórico de la Nobleza.

Aram, Bethany, and Bartolomé Yun-Casalilla, eds. *Global Goods and the Spanish Empire, 1492–1824: Circulation, Resistance and Diversity.* Palgrave Macmillan, 2014.

Autos entre partes. 1624. Archivo General de Indias, Casa de la Contratación.

– 1633. Archivo General de Indias, Casa de la Contratación.

– 1634. Archivo General de Indias, Casa de la Contratación.

Autos entre partes de 1676. 1676. Archivo General de Indias, Casa de la Contratación.

Autos fiscales. 1687. Archivo General de Indias, Casa de la Contratación.

Avellaneda, Francisco de. "La boda de Juan Rana." *Rasgos del ocio en diferentes bayles, entremeses y loas, de diversos autores,* vol. 2, Domingo García Morras, 1664, pp. 25–33. Biblioteca Nacional de España.

Barrientos, Antonio. "Mojiganga de las beatas." *Rasgos del ocio en diferentes bayles, entremeses y loas, de diversos autores,* vol. 2, Domingo García Morras, 1664, pp. 11–24. Biblioteca Nacional de España.

Barrionuevo, Jerónimo de. *Avisos de Don Jerónimo de Barrionuevo (1654–1658).* Edited by Antonio Paz y Melia, vol. 2, Atlas, 1969.

Barrios, Juan de. *Verdadera medicina, cirugía y astrología.* Fernando Balli, Mexico City, 1607.

Bauer-Funke, Cerstin. "La función simbólica y escenográfica de la comida en el teatro del Siglo de Oro." *Teatro español del Siglo de Oro; Teoría y práctica,* 1998, pp. 27–37.

Bender, Margaret. "Reflections on What Writing Means, beyond What It 'Says': The Political Economy and Semiotics of Graphic Pluralism in the Americas." *Ethnohistory,* vol. 57, no. 1, 2010, pp. 175–82.

Bletter, Nathaniel, and Douglas C. Daly. "Cacao and Its Relatives in South America." McNeil, pp. 31–68.

Bolles, David. *A Translation of the Edited Text of Ritual of the Bacabs.* Labyrinthos, 2003, http://davidsbooks.org/www/Bacabs.pdf.

Bricker, Victoria R. "Bilingualism in the Maya Codices and the Books of Chilam Balam of Chumayel." *Written Language and Literacy,* vol. 3, 2000, pp. 77–115.

Bristol, John, and Matthew Restall. "Potions and Perils: Love-Magic in Seventeenth-Century Afro-Mexico and Afro-Yucatan." *Black Mexico: Race and Society from Colonial to Modern Times,* edited by Ben Vinson and Matthew Restall, U of New Mexico P, 2009, pp. 155–79.

Brulotte, Ronda L., and Alvin Starkman. "Caldo de Piedra and Claiming Pre-Hispanic Cuisine as Cultural Heritage." *Edible Identities: Food as Cultural Heritage,* edited by Ronda L. Brulotte and Michael A. Di Giovine, Ashgate Publishing Company, 2014, pp. 109–23.

Bustamante, Jesús. "La atracción de lo raro y peregrino." *Relación de la Nueva España,* Polifemo, 1986, pp. 9–69.

Calderón de la Barca, Pedro. *El pésame de la viuda: Mojiganga.* Biblioteca Virtual Miguel de Cervantes, 2000, http://www.cervantesvirtual.com/nd/ark:/59851/bmc08647.

- *Entremés famoso de las lenguas*. Biblioteca Virtual Miguel de Cervantes, 2014.
- *Entremés de la rabia*. Biblioteca Virtual Miguel de Cervantes, 2000, http://www.cervantesvirtual.com/obra/la-rabia-entremes--0/.
- *Gustos y disgustos son no más que imaginación*. Biblioteca Virtual Miguel de Cervantes, 2014, http://www.cervantesvirtual.com/obra/gustos-y-disgustos-son-no-mas-que-imaginacion-0/.
- *La garapiña*. Edited by Evangelina Rodríguez and Antonio Tordera, Biblioteca Virtual Miguel de Cervantes, 2000.
- "Mojiganga de las lenguas." *Obras teatrales de Calderón de La Barca y de otros autores*, edited by Pedro Carranza, 1706, pp. 43–7. Biblioteca Nacional de España.
Calderón de la Barca, Pedro, and Agustín Moreto. "Baile del chocolatero." *Colección de bailes, mojigangas, entremeses y coplas*, eighteenth century, pp. 196–200, Biblioteca Nacional de España, http://bdh.bne.es/bnesearch/detalle/bdh0000216378.
Cáncer y Velasco, Gerónimo de. *Manojito de entremeses, a diferentes asuntos, de bailes, y mojigangas*. 1700.
Cárdenas, Juan de. *Problemas y secretos maravillosos de las Indias*. Vol. 9, Ediciones cultural hispánica, 1945.
Caro Mallén de Soto, Ana. *Valor, agravio y mujer*. Association for Hispanic Classical Theatre, http://www.comedias.org/caro/valagr.pdf. Accessed 21 November 2017.
Carvajal y Saavedra, Mariana de. *Navidades de Madrid y noches entretenidas, en ocho novelas*. Edited by Catherine Soriano, Comunidad de Madrid, 1993.
Castillo Solórzano, Alonso de. *El mayorazgo figura*. Biblioteca Virtual Miguel de Cervantes, 2001, http://www.cervantesvirtual.com/obra/el-mayorazgo-figura--1/.
Castro, Francisco de. "Doña Parba Materia." *Alegría cómica*, vol. 3, 1702, pp. 59–73. Biblioteca Nacional de España.
- "Entremés del figurón." *Alegría cómica*, vol. 3, 1702, fol. 1–13. Biblioteca Nacional de España.
Cervantes Saavedra, Miguel de. "Novela de la gitanilla." *Novelas ejemplares I*, edited by Harry Sieber, vol. 1, Cátedra, 1980, pp. 59–134.
Coe, Sophie D., and Michael D. Coe. *The True History of Chocolate*. Thames and Hudson, 1996.
Colmenero de Ledesma, Antonio. *Curioso tratado de la naturaleza y calidad del chocolate*. Francisco Martínez, 1631, http://bdh-rd.bne.es/viewer.vm?id=0000090098&page=1.
Colón, Cristóbal. *Diario del descubrimiento*. Edited by Manuel Alvar, vol. 2, La Muralla, 1976.

– *Textos y documentos completos: Relaciones de viajes, cartas y memoriales.*
Edited by Consuelo Varela Bueno, Alianza, 1982.

Colón, Fernando. *Historia del almirante Don Cristóbal Colón, por su hijo Don
Hernando; Traducida nuevamente del italiano.* Translated by Manuel Serrano
y Sanz, vol. 1, General de Victoriano Suárez, 1932.

– *Historia del almirante Don Cristóbal Colón, por su hijo Don Hernando;
Traducida nuevamente del italiano.* Translated by Manuel Serrano y Sanz,
vol. 2, General de Victoriano Suárez, 1932.

Conquistador anónimo and Jesús Bustamante. *Relación de la Nueva España:
Texto bilingüe.* Ed. Polifemo, 1986.

"Consulta original de los médicos de orden de Madrid sobre el chocolate."
Papeles varios, 1666, pp. 284–5. Biblioteca de Castilla-La Mancha.

Coplas nuevas para que sepan del modo que se toma el chocolate. 1801, http://
bdh-rd.bne.es/viewer.vm?id=0000077833&page=1.

Correas, Gonzalo. *Vocabulario de refranes y frases proverbiales y otras
formulas comunes de la lengua castellana en que van todos los impresos antes
y otra gran copia.* Jaime Ratés, 1906, https://archive.org/details
/vocabularioderef00corruoft.

Cortés, Hernán. *Cartas de relación.* Edited by Mario Hernández, Historia 16,
1985.

Cortijo Herraiz, Thomas. *Discurso apologético médico astronómico: Pruébase
la real influencia de los cuerpos celestes en estos sublunares, y la necesidad de
la observancia de sus aspectos para el mas recto uso de la medicina: Con un
examen sobre el uso de el chocolate en las enfermedades.* Eugenio García de
Honorato y San Miguel, 1729. Biblioteca Nacional de España.

Craveri, Michela E. *Popol Vuh. Herramienta para un estudio crítico del texto
k'iche'.* Universidad nacional autónoma de México, 2013.

Cruz, Ramón de la. "Las dos viuditas." *Teatro, ó coleccion de los saynetes y
demas obras dramáticas*, vol. 5, Imprenta Real, 1788, pp. 303–40.

– *Las tertulias de Madrid o El porqué de las tertulias.* Biblioteca Virtual Miguel
de Cervantes, 2002, http://www.cervantesvirtual.com/obra/las-tertulias-de
-madrid-o-el-porque-de-las-tertulias--0/.

Cuenca, Ambrosio de. *A igual agravio, no hay duelo.* Biblioteca Virtual Miguel
de Cervantes, 2010, http://www.cervantesvirtual.com/obra/a-igual-agravio
-no-ay-duelo/.

Cull, John T. "'Ese paso está ya hecho': Calderón's Observations on *Corral*
Performances." *Forum for Modern Language Studies*, vol. 29, no. 3, 1993,
pp. 271–86.

Curiel, Gustavo. "Glosario." *Juan Correa: Su vida y su obra*, edited by Elias
Vargas Lugo and Gustavo Curiel, vol. 3, Universidad nacional autónoma de
México, 1991, pp. 271–302.

de Durand-Forest, Jacqueline. "El cacao entre los aztecas." *Estudios de cultura náhuatl*, vol. 7, 1967, pp. 155–81.

Día-Plaja, Fernando. *La vida cotidiana en la España del Siglo de Oro*. Editorial EDAF, 1994.

Díaz Balsera, Viviana. "Erasing the Pyramid under the Cross: Motolinía's History of the Indians of New Spain and the Construction of the Nahua Christian Subject." *Journal of Spanish Cultural Studies*, vol. 4, no. 1, 2003, pp. 111–23.

Díaz Bravo, José Vincente. *El ayuno reformado segun practica de la primitiva iglesia por los cinco breves de Benedicto XIV: Obra historica, canonico-medica con noticia particular de los privilegios, que gozan en España los soldados y una disertacion historica, medico-chymica de el chocolate, y su uso*. Pasqual Ibañez, 1754.

Díaz del Castillo, Bernal. *Historia verdadera de la conquista de la Nueva España*. Edited by Guillero Serés, Real Academia Española, 2011.

– *The History of the Conquest of New Spain by Bernal Díaz Del Castillo*. Translated by David Carrasco, U of New Mexico P, 2008. *EBSCOhost*, search.ebscohost.com/login.aspx?direct=true&db=nlebk&AN=238348&site=eds-live&scope=site.

Diccionario de autoridades. Real Academia Española. Vols. 1–6. Impr. de D. Joachin Ibarra, 1726–39. https://webfrl.rae.es/DA.html.

Díez Borque, José María. *La sociedad española y los viajeros del siglo XVII*. Selecciones Gráficas, 1975.

Díez de Aux de Armendáriz, Lope. *Sobre depósito de cacao en la alhóndiga*. 1638. Archivo Histórico Nacional.

Dillinger, Teresa L., et al. "Food of the Gods: Cure for Humanity? A Cultural History of the Medicinal and Ritual Use of Chocolate." *Journal of Nutrition*, vol. 130, no. 8, August 2000, pp. 2057S–2072S.

Domingo, Xavier. "La cocina precolombina en España." *Conquista y comida: Consecuencias del encuentro de dos mundos*. 3rd edition, edited by Janet Long, Universidad nacional autónoma de México, 2018, pp. 15–30, http://www.historicas.unam.mx/publicaciones/publicadigital/libros/323/323_06_03_cocinaprecolombina.pdf.

Domingo Víctor de la Cruz, Felipe IV. *Por quanto se ha entendido, que de algun tiempo a esta parte se han introducido por los puertos destos mis reynos muchas cantidades de cacao fuera de registro, en contravencion de mis reales ordenes*. 29 October 1620. Sala Cervantes, Biblioteca Nacional de España.

Durán, Diego. *Historia de las Indias de Nueva-España y Islas de Tierra Firme*. Vol. 1, Impr. de J.M. Andrade y F. Escalante, 1867.

– *Historia de las Indias de Nueva-España y Islas de Tierra Firme*. Vol. 2, Impr. de J.M. Andrade y F. Escalante, 1880.

– *The Aztecs: The History of the Indies of New Spain*. Translated by Doris Heyden and Fernando Horcasitas, Orion P, 1964.

Earle, Rebecca. "Spaniards, Cannibals, and the Eucharist in the New World." *To Feast on Us as Their Prey: Cannibalism and the Early Modern Atlantic*, edited by Rachel B. Herrmann, U of Arkansas P, 2019, pp. 81–96.

– *The Body of the Conquistador: Food, Race and the Colonial Experience in Spanish America, 1492–1700*. Cambridge UP, 2012.

– "Diet, Travel, and Colonialism in the Early Modern World." *Global Goods and the Spanish Empire, 1492–1824: Circulation, Resistance and Diversity*, edited by Bethany Aram and Bartolomé Yun-Casalilla, Palgrave Macmillan, 2014, pp. 137–52.

"El nigromántico." *Fiesta burlesca que se representó á su magestad [D. Carlos II] el día veinte de febrero, en la villa de la Torre de Esteban Hambrán, año de mil seiscientos y ochenta y cinco*, 1685, pp. 22–6. Biblioteca Nacional de España.

Emmart, Emily Walcott. *The Badianus Manuscript (Codex Barberini, Latin 241) Vatican Library, an Aztec Herbal of 1552*. Johns Hopkins UP, 1940.

Entremés del duelo del vejete. Biblioteca Virtual Miguel de Cervantes, 2013, http://www.cervantesvirtual.com/obra/entremes-del-duelo-del-vejete/.

Entremeses varios ahora nuevamente recogidos de los mejores ingenios de España. Los herederos de Diego Dormer, 1650. Biblioteca Nacional de España.

Fattacciu, Irene. "Cacao: From an Exotic Curiosity to a Spanish Commodity. The Diffusion of New Patterns of Consumption in Eighteenth-Century Spain." *Food and History*, vol. 7, no. 1, 2009, pp. 53–78.

Fernández de Madrigal, Francisco. *Carta sobre los derechos del cacao, chocolate y azúcares*. 17 December 1682. Archivo General de Indias.

Fernández de Oviedo, Gonzalo. *Historia general y natural de las Indias*. Vol. 1, Ediciones Atlas, 1959.

Fernández-de-Pinedo, Nadia. "Global Commodities in Early Modern Spain." *Global History and New Polycentric Approaches: Europe, Asia and the Americas in a World Network System*, edited by Manuel Pérez García and Lucio De Sousa, Palgrave Macmillan, 2018, pp. 293–318.

Fernández de Portocarrero, Luis Manuel. *Edicto en que se manda prohibir el almorzar, comer, merendar, bever, tomar chocolate, ù otros qualesquier refrescos, ò colaciones en las iglesias, capillas, hermitas, oratorios, assi publicos, como privados, y en otros lugares sagrados de nuestro arçobispado*. 1681.

Fertig, Christine, and Ulrich Pfister. "Coffee, Mind and Body: Global Material Culture and the Eighteenth-Century Hamburg Import Trade." Gerritsen and Riello, pp. 221–40.

Findlen, Paula. "How (Early Modern) Things Travel." Gerritsen and Riello, pp. 241–6.

Freidel, David, et al. *Maya Cosmos: Three Thousand Years on the Shaman's Path*. William Morrow and Company, 1993.

Gamboa, Yolanda. "Consuming the Other, Creating the Self: The Cultural Implications of the Aztecs' Chocolate from Tirso de Molina to Agustín Moreto and Pedro Lanini y Sagredo." *Crosscurrents: Transatlantic Perspectives on Early Modern Hispanic Drama*, edited by Mindy Badía and Bonnie L Gasior, Rosemont Publishing and Printing Corp, 2006, pp. 25–39.

García Garzón, Juan Ignacio. "Mestiza." *Clásicas críticas*, 18 June 2018, http://clasicascriticas.blogspot.es/1529319772/mestiza/.

García Icazbalceta, Joaquín, and Toribio de Benavente Motolinia. "Introducción." *Memoriales e historia de los indios de la Nueva España*, 1903.

Gasco, Janine. "Cacao and Economic Inequality in Colonial Soconusco, Chiapas, Mexico." *Journal of Anthropological Research*, vol. 52, no. 4, 1996, pp. 385–409. *JSTOR*, www.jstor.org/stable/3630294.

Gascón, Christopher D. "Erasure, Exoticism, Hybridity: Cultural Alterity in Santa Rosa Del Perú." *Crosscurrents: Transatlantic Perspectives on Early Modern Hispanic Drama*, edited by Mindy Badía and Bonnie L Gasior, Rosemont Publishing and Printing Corp, 2006, pp. 40–63.

Gerritsen, Anne, and Giorgio Riello. *The Global Lives of Things: The Material Culture of Connections in the Early Modern World*. Routledge, 2016.

Goetz, Delia, and Sylvanus Griswold Morley, translators. *Popul Vuh: The Book of the Ancient Maya*. Dover Publications, 2003.

González, Olympia B. "Alimento y mujer en un poema de Antonio Hurtado de Mendoza." *Calíope: Journal of the Society for Renaissance and Baroque Hispanic Poetry*, vol. 6, no. 1–2, 2000, pp. 237–50.

González de la Vara, Martín. "Origen y virtudes del chocolate." *Conquista y comida: Consecuencias del encuentro de dos mundos*, edited by Janet Long, Universidad nacional autónoma de México, 1996, pp. 291–308.

González Quiroz, Mabel. *Relación verdadera del gran sermón: Edición y estudio: Chocolate e inquisición en un manuscrito satírico sefardí*. Paso de Barca, 2015.

González-Echevarría, Roberto. *Celestina's Brood: Continuities of the Baroque in Spanish and Latin American Literature*. Duke UP, 1993.

The Good Huswifes Handmaide for the Kitchin. Richard Jones, 1594. Edited by Sam Wallace, 2011, *Justus Liebig Universitat Giessen*, http://www.staff.uni-giessen.de/gloning/ghhk/.

Govantes, Diego de. "Entremés famoso del calcetero indiano." *Pensil ameno de entremeses. Escritos por los ingenios más clásicos de España*, Juan Micón, Impresor del Reino, 1691, pp. 87–96. Biblioteca Nacional de España.

Greer, Margaret R. *Manos teatrales*. https://www.manos.net/. Accessed 16 June 2018.

Grivetti, Louis Evan, and Howard-Yana Shapiro, editors. *Chocolate: History, Culture, and Heritage*. Wiley and Sons, 2009.

Hernández de Toledo, Francisco. *Cuatro libros de la naturaleza, y virtudes de las plantas, y animales que están en la Nueva España, y la método y corrección, y preparación, que para administrarlas se requiere con lo que el doctor Francisco Hernández escribió en lengua latina*. Translated by Francisco Ximenez, Casa de la viuda de Diego López Dávalos, 1615, http://bibdigital.rjb.csic.es/spa/Libro.php?Libro=4961&Pagina=1.

– *Historia de las plantas de Nueva España*. Vol. 3, Imprenta Universitaria, 1946.

Hernández Morejón, Antonio. *Historia bibliográfica de la medicina española*. Vol. 4, Imprenta de la viuda de Jordan e hijos, 1846.

Herrero García, Miguel. *La vida española en el siglo XVII: Las bebidas*. Vol. 1, Gráficas Universal, 1933.

Heyden, Doris, and Ana María L. Velasco. "Aves van, aves vienen: El guajolote, la gallina y el pato." *Conquista y comida: Consecuencias del encuentro de dos mundos*, 3rd edition, edited by Janet Long, Universidad nacional autónoma de México, 2019, pp. 237–54, http://www.historicas.unam.mx/publicaciones/publicadigital/libros/323/323_06_17_avesvan.pdf.

Huerta, Javier. "Mestiza." *Clásicas críticas*, 18 June 2018, http://clasicascriticas.blogspot.es/1529322177/mestiza/.

Hurst, William Jeffrey, et al. "Archaeology: Cacao Usage by the Earliest Maya Civilization." *Nature*, vol. 418, July 2002, pp. 289–90.

Hurtado de Mendoza, Antonio. *Obras poéticas de Antonio Hurtado de Mendoza*. Edited by Rafael Benítez Claros, vol. 2, Gráficas Ultra, 1948.

– *Obras poéticas de Antonio Hurtado de Mendoza*. Vol. 3, Gráficas Ultra, 1948.

Hurtado, Tomás. *Chocolate y tabaco, ayuno eclesiástico y natural*. Francisco García, 1645, http://digibug.ugr.es/handle/10481/5117#.VeWyYdNViko.

Indice del acuerdo, que el reyno hizo eligiendo medios generales en lugar de los arbitrios particulares de que usauan los lugares, para la paga del seruicio de los dos millones y medio, y las administraciones que para su cobrança se dieron. 1634. Biblioteca Nacional de España, Sala Cervantes.

Jurado Santos, Agapita. *Obras teatrales derivadas de las novelas cervantinas (siglo XVII): Para una bibliografía*. Reichenberger, 2005.

Knowlton, Timothy. "Literacy and Healing: Semiotic Ideologies and the Entextualization of Colonial Maya Medical Incantations." *Ethnohistory*, vol. 62, no. 3, 2015, pp. 573–95.

Kufer, Johanna, and Cameron L. McNeil. "The Jaguar Tree (*Theobroma Bicolor Bonpl*)." McNeil, pp. 90–104.

Lafuente, Javier, and Lucía Abellán. "España rechaza con firmeza la exigencia de México de pedir perdón por los abusos de la conquista." *El País*, 26 March 2019, https://elpais.com/internacional/2019/03/25/mexico/1553539019_249884.html.

Landa, Diego de. *Relación de las cosas de Yucatán*. Edited by Miguel Rivera Dorado, Dastin, 1985.

Lardizabal, Vicente D. *Memoria sobre las utilidades de el chocolate. Para precaber las incomodidades, que resulta del uso de las aguas minerales, y promover sus buenos efectos, como los de los purgantes, y otros remedios: Y para curar ciertas dolencias*. Antonio Castilla, 1788. Biblioteca Nacional de España.

Leon Pinelo, Antonio de. *Questión moral: Si el chocolate quebranta el ayuno eclesiástico*. Viuda de Juan González, 1636, google books.

López, Tomás, and Cristóbal Pérez de Herrera. *Privilegios y policía de Madrid en los reinados de Felipe III, Felipe IV y Carlos II*. 1601–1700. Sala Cervantes.

Marradón, Bartolomé. *Du chocolat: Dialogue entre un medecin, un indien & un bourgeois*. 1618. Sala Cervantes.

Martín Sánchez, Manuel. *Seres míticos y personajes fantásticos españoles*. Editorial EDAF, 2002.

Mata, Juan de la. *Arte de repostería, en que se contiene todo género de hacer dulces secos, y en líquido, bizcochos, turrones y natas … Con una breve instrucción para conocer las frutas, y servirlas crudas, y diez mezas*. Antonio Marin, 1747. Biblioteca Nacional de España.

Matos Fragoso, Juan de. "La fregona." *Autos sacramentales: Con quatro comedias nuevas y sus loas y entremeses*, vol. 1, Maria de Quiñones, a costa de Juan de Valdes, 1655, pp. 11–14r. Biblioteca Nacional de España.

Maura y Gamazo, Gabriel. *Carlos II y su corte*. F. Beltrán, 1911.

– *Supersticiones de los siglos XVI y XVII y hechizos de Carlos II*. Saturnino Calleja, 1920.

McNeil, Cameron L., editor. *Chocolate in Mesoamerica: A Cultural History of Cacao*. UP of Florida, 2006.

Miguel Magro, Tania de. "A Study of Women's Intelligence in Moreto's *No puede ser*." *Bulletin of the Comediantes*, vol. 62, no. 1, 2010, pp. 79–102.

– *El calcetero indiano*. 1 July 2020.

Mignolo, Walter. *The Darker Side of the Renaissance*. U of Michigan P, 1995.

Milini, Sabo. *Edicto de Don Sabo Milini, nuncio apostolico en España, prohibiendo tomar chocolate, almorzar, comer y beber en las iglesias, a cualquier clase de personas, condicion y categoría*. 1681.

Mir, Miguel. "Al lector." *Vocabulario de refranes y frases proverbiales y otras fórmulas comunes de la lengua castellana en que van todos los impresos antes*

y otra gran copia, by Gonzalo Correas, Jaime Ratés, 1906, pp. v–xiii, https://
ia600907.us.archive.org/9/items/vocabularioderef00corruoft
/vocabularioderef00corruoft_bw.pdf.

Molina, Tirso de. *Amazonas en las Indias*. Biblioteca Virtual Miguel de
Cervantes, 1999, http://www.cervantesvirtual.com/obra/amazonas-en-las
-indias--0/.

– *La villana de Vallecas*. Francisco Lyra, 1627, http://www.comedias.org/tirso
/villana_de_vallecas.pdf.

Monteser, Francisco de. *Entremés de la hidalguía*. Biblioteca Virtual Miguel de
Cervantes, 2012, http://www.cervantesvirtual.com/obra/entremes-de-la
-hidalguia/.

Moreto, Agustín. *La ocasión hace al ladrón, y truque de las maletas*. Biblioteca
Virtual Miguel de Cervantes, 2013, http://www.cervantesvirtual.com/obra/la
-ocasion-hace-al-ladron--comedia-famosa/.

– *No puede ser el guardar una mujer*. Biblioteca Virtual Miguel de Cervantes,
2013, http://www.cervantesvirtual.com/obra/comedia-no-puede-ser-guardar
-una-muger/.

Moreto, Agustín, and Gerónimo de Cáncer. *La fuerza del natural*. Biblioteca
Virtual Miguel de Cervantes, 2013, http://www.cervantesvirtual.com/obra
/comedia-famosa-la-fuerza-del-natural/.

Moreto, Agustín, and Pedro Lanini y Sagredo. *Santa Rosa del Perú*. Lingkua,
2014.

Moss, Sarah. *Chocolate: A Global History*. Reaktion Books, 2009.

Motolinia, Toribio. *Memoriales e historia de los indios de la Nueva España*.
Edited by Fidel de Lejarza, Atlas, 1970.

Nadeau, Carolyn. *Food Matters: Alonso Quijano's Diet and the Discourse of
Food in Early Modern Spain*. U of Toronto P, 2016.

Nebrija, Antonio de. *Gramática de la lengua castellana*. Linkgua, 2009.
EBSCOhost, search.ebscohost.com/login.aspx?direct=true&db=nlebk&AN
=264291&site=eds-live&scope=site.

Nieto-Cuebas, Glenda Y. "Amazons in the Indies or Witches in the Amazon?
Representing Otherness through the Stereotype of the Witch." *Female
Amerindians in Early Modern Spanish Theater*, edited by Gladys Robalino,
Bucknell UP, 2014, pp. 39–59.

Norton, Marcy. *Sacred Gifts, Profane Pleasures: A History of Tobacco and
Chocolate in the Atlantic World*. Cornell UP, 2008.

Olmedo, Alonso de. *Entremés de las locas caseras*. Biblioteca Virtual Miguel de
Cervantes, 2013, http://www.cervantesvirtual.com/obra/entremes-de-las
-locas-caseras/.

*Papeles Varios. Comprehende diferentes papeles sobre asumptos de comercio,
fabricas, &*. 1696–1738.

Pérez, Mirzam C. *The Comedia of Virginity: Mary and the Politics of Seventeenth-Century Spanish Theater*. Baylor UP, 2012.

Pérez Samper, María de los Ángeles. "The Early Modern Food Revolution: A Perspective from the Iberian Atlantic." *Global Goods and the Spanish Empire, 1492–1824: Circulation, Resistance and Diversity*, edited by Bethany Aram and Bartolomé Yun-Casalilla, Palgrave Macmillan, 2014, pp. 17–37.

Perry, Mary Elizabeth. *Gender and Disorder in Early Modern Seville*. Princeton UP, 1990.

Piperi, Geronimo, and Thomas Cortijo Herraiz. "Décima glosada al chocolate." *Discurso apologético médico astronómico: Pruébase la real influencia de los cuerpos celestes en estos sublunares, y la necessidad de la observancia de sus aspectos para el mas recto uso de la medicina: Con un examen sobre el uso de el chocolate en las enfermedades*, Eugenio Garcia de Honorato y San Miguel, 1729, pp. 116–19. Biblioteca Nacional de España.

Poesías satíricas varias. 1759. Biblioteca Nacional de España.

Quevedo, Francisco de. *Poderoso caballero*. Biblioteca Virtual Universal, 2003.

Quevedo, Francisco de, and James O. Crosby. *Nuevas cartas de la última prisión de Quevedo*. Tamesis Books, 2005.

Quevedo, Francisco de, and Ernesto Pérez Zúñiga. *Discurso de todos los diablos, infierno enmendado, o El entremetido y la dueña*. Celeste Ediciones, 1998.

Quiñones de Benavente, Luis. "Don Gaiferos." *Colección de entremeses, loas, bailes, jácaras y mojigangas desde fines del siglo XVI a mediados del XVII*, edited by Emilio Cotarelo y Mori, vol. 18, Bailly-Baillière, 1911, pp. 611–13.

– *Entremés cantado de el mago*. Biblioteca Virtual Miguel de Cervantes, 2002, http://www.cervantesvirtual.com/obra/el-mago-entremes-cantado--0/.

– *Entremés de la constreñida*. Biblioteca Virtual Miguel de Cervantes, 2013, http://www.cervantesvirtual.com/obra/entremes-de-la-constrenida/.

Quirós, Francisco de Bernardo. *El sordo: Entremés*. 1700–1601, http://bdh.bne.es/bnesearch/detalle/bdh0000232795.

Rípodas Ardenaz, Daisy. "Visión de América en el teatro de santos indianos auriseculares." *Teatro: Revista de Estudios Teatrales*, vol. 15, 2001, pp. 129–42.

Robertson, Emma. *Chocolate, Women and Empire: A Social and Cultural History*. Manchester UP, 2009.

Rodríguez, Evangelina. "Editing Theater: A Strategy for Reading, an Essay about Dramaturgy." *The Politics of Editing*, edited by Nicholas Spadaccini and Jenaro Talens, U of Minnesota P, 1992, pp. 95–109.

Rodríguez, Evangelina, and Antonio Tordera. *Calderón y la obra corta dramática del siglo XVII*. Tamesis Books, 1983.

Romero, Sergio. "Language, Catechisms, and Mesoamerican Lords in Highland Guatemala: Addressing 'God' after the Spanish Conquest." *Ethnohistory*, vol. 62, no. 3, 2015, pp. 623–49.

Romero Asenjo, Rafael. *El bodegón español en el siglo XVII: Desvelando Su Naturaleza Oculta*. Icono I&R, 2009.

Roys, Ralph L. *Ritual of the Bacabs*. U of Oklahoma P, 1965.

Sahagún, Bernardo de. *Historia general de las cosas de Nueva España*. Edited by Juan Carlos Temprano, vol. 2, Historia 16, 1990.

Salas Barbadillo, Alonso Jerónimo de. *El sagaz Estacio, marido examinado*. Biblioteca Virtual Miguel de Cervantes, 1999, http://www.cervantesvirtual .com/obra/el-sagaz-estacio-marido-examinado--0/.

Sampeck, Kathryn E. "Introduction: Colonial Mesoamerican Literacy." *Ethnohistory*, vol. 62, no. 3, 2015, pp. 409–20.

– "Pipil Writing: An Archaeology of Prototypes and a Political Economy of Literacy." *Ethnohistory*, vol. 62, no. 3, 2015, pp. 469–95.

Santos, Francisco, and Enrique Suárez Figaredo. "Día y noche de Madrid." *Lemir*, vol. 14, 2010, pp. 629–796.

Sarabia Viejo, María Justina, and Isabel Arenas Frutos. "¿Olla común? El problema de la alimentación en la reforma monacal femenina. México, siglo XVIII." *Los sabores de España y América. Cultura y alimentación*, edited by Antonio Garrido Aranda, La Val de Onsera, 1999, pp. 247–67.

Saville, Marshall, translator. *Narrative of Some Things of New Spain and the Great City of Temistatan Mexico*. Cortes Society, 1917.

Shaw, W.A. *The History of Currency 1252 to 1894*. 2nd ed., Burt Franklin, 1966.

Smith, Pamela H. "Itineraries of Materials and Knowledge in the Early Modern World." *The Global Lives of Things: The Material Culture of Connections in the Early Modern World*. Gerritsen and Riello, pp. 31–61.

Soria, Julieta. *Mestiza*. Performances by Gloria Muñoz and Julián Ortega, Emilia Yagüe Producciones Company, 14 June 2018, Teatro Salón Cervantes, Alcalá de Henares, Spain.

Tedlock, Dennis, translator. *Popol Vuh: The Mayan Book of the Dawn of Life*. Simon and Schuster, 1996.

Tejera, Juan Francisco de. *La rueda y los buñuelos*. Biblioteca Virtual Miguel de Cervantes, 2013.

Thompson, Alyse. "Report: Valentine's Day Third Best Holiday for Chocolate Candy Sales." *Candy Industry*, February 2018, https://www.candyindustry .com/articles/88062-report-valentines-day-third-best-holiday-for-chocolate -candy-sales.

Thompson, John Eric Sidney. *A Commentary on the Dresden Codex: A Maya Hieroglyphic Book*. American Philosophical Society, 1972.

Torquemada, Juan de. *Monarquía indiana*. Vol. 2, Porrua, 1969.

Torres, Castro de. *Panegírico al chocolate*. 2nd ed., E. Rasco, 1887.

Vail, Gabrielle, and Christine Hernández. *The Maya Codices Database*. Version 4.1, 2013, http://www.mayacodices.org.

Valverde Turices, Santiago de. *Discurso del chocolate (o de una bebida que aunque en las Indias haya sido antigua, en este lugar es mas nueva)*. J. Cabrera, 1625. Biblioteca Nacional de España.

Varey, Simon, editor. *The Mexican Treasury: The Writings of Dr. Francisco Hernández*. Translated by Rafael Chabrán et al., Stanford UP, 2000.

Vega Carpio, Lope de. *La Dorotea*. Edited by Donald McGrady, Real Academia Española, 2011.

– *La famosa comedia del nuevo mundo descubierto por Cristóbal Colón*. Edited by Ricardo Castells, Association for Hispanic Classical Theatre, http://www.comedias.org/lope/NMundo.pdf. Accessed 1 December 2019.

Wilkinson, Alexander Samuel, and Alejandra Ulla Lorenzo, editors. *Iberian Books/Libros ibéricos*. Vols. 2 and 3, Brill, 2015.

Zafra, Antonio de, editor. *Floresta de entremeses y rasgos del ocio, a diferentes asuntos, de bailes y mogigangas*. Antonio de Zafra en casa de Juan Fernández, 1691. Biblioteca Nacional de España.

Zarrillo, Sonia, et al. "The Use and Domestication of Theobroma Cacao during the Mid-Holocene in the Upper Amazon." *Nature Ecology and Evolution*, vol. 2, 2018, pp. 1879–88.

Zayas, María de. *Desengaños amorosos*. 4th edition, edited by Alicia Yllera, Cátedra, 2000.

Index

Toronto Iberic